MW01055199

11 Simple Tools to Survive Your First Year in the Air Force

Copyright 2015 ©

All Rights Reserved

Disclaimer

Contents

Introduction

If you are planning on joining the Air Force then there is certainly a lot that you need to know. The Air Force has made some major changes in the past decade. It's not the same as it might have been for your parents, grandparents, or other role models whom you may look up to. The main difference is the manner in which the Air Force turns civilians into Airmen.

An emphasis is being placed on toughening up recruits by raising the physical fitness standards. Some of the classroom training has been replaced by combat training and chemical/biological weapon defense. These changes have caused the length of basic training to be increased by 2 weeks.

With that said, basic training seems to be the most intimidating aspect of joining the Air Force. However, there is much more of a transition than basic training. So many new cadets make it through basic training only to discover that life after basic training is even more difficult. The transition between civilian life and military life is not an easy one.

This book will show you how to make this transition go as smoothly as possible. I'm going to take you through this transition and give you some tips that will help push you in the right direction. Are you ready to get started?

Chapter 1

What to Know Before you Sign

There are a few key things that you need to know before you commit your life to the service of the United States of America. Make no mistake either. As a member of the Air Force, you will be expected to make some huge sacrifices for your country. Here's what you need to know before you sign on the dotted lines.

Enlistment Incentives

The Air Force receives more applications that any other branch of the military – so many that they cannot accept them all. They are in high demand so there are very few enlistment incentives. In fact, only a few critical jobs offer an incentive bonus. The Air Force does provide a College Loan Repayment Program and offers an enlistment rank up to E-3 for those who have college credits and have graduated from JROTC.

Finally, the Air Force promotes those who enlist for at least six years at an accelerated rate. All-in-all, the Air Force is so popular that they don't need to offer incentives in order to recruit.

Air Force Job Opportunities are Fair to All Members!

There are over 150 enlisted jobs available in the Air Force,

What to Know Before you Sign

with only three being closed to women. Those three jobs are Tactical Air Combat and Control, Combat Controller, and Pararescue. Enlisted jobs with the Air Force are formally known as "Air Force Specialty Codes" (AFSCs). Let's look at the two types of job programs offered by the Air Force:

Guaranteed Job

The Guaranteed Job program does just as the name implies; it guarantees that the applicant is trained in a specific Air Force job.

Guaranteed Aptitude

Under this program, the Air Force guarantees that the applicant is selected for a job that applies to one of the designed aptitude categories. There are four aptitude areas in the Air Force:

> ➢ Electronic

> ➢ Mechanical

> ➢ Administrative

> ➢ General

In order to make things fair for all recruits, the Air Force generally distributes their enlistment contracts at a 40:60 guaranteed job ratio. In other words, 40% of jobs are made available for Guaranteed Job contracts while 60% are reserved for Guaranteed Aptitude contracts.

Putting It All Together

That's a lot of technical details so now it's time to break them own into an easily digestible format. Here's a step-by-step look at how the process works.

1. An applicant travels to their local Military Entrance Processing Station (MEPS).

2. The applicant will then take a medical examination, undergo the ASVAB, and meet with a specialist who determines their qualifications.

3. The applicant will then meet an Air Force Job Counselor, who has access to the list of jobs open through the Air Force. One of two things happens at this point:

> ➢ The counselor finds a job that the applicant is qualified for.

> ➢ There are no jobs currently available. Therefore, the applicant will fill out a list of preferred jobs (along with one aptitude area) and then enlists in the Delayed Enlistment Program.

4. When/if a job is available, the applicant is assigned to that area.

5. Applicant is given a basic training shipping date.

6. If enlisted through a Guaranteed Aptitude Program, then an applicant will have to meet with a job councilor during their second week at basic training. They are given a list of available jobs to choose from. Applicants have one week to choose.

My point here is that if you are planning to enlist in the Air Force, then you must be very flexible with job assignments. Many recruiters will actually refuse to process an applicant if they seem to be locked on a single job. In fact, most recruiters will have a checklist that the applicant must sign before shipping to MEPS. This checklist verifies that the applicant is not joining the Air Force in order to "Job Shop".

Job flexibility is a requirement. Sometimes the Air Force will work a person in an area outside of the job they were trained in. This only happens when they are in a bind to fill a position but you need to be aware that you might not get the job you want.

Frequently Asked Questions from People Just Like You

What are the age requirements for joining the Air Force?

Applicants who have never been in the service must be in enrolled by the age of 28.

Applicants for commissioned officer training programs like physicians, nurses, and other health provider positions must be enrolled in training before age 40.

11 Simple Tools to Survive your First Year in the Air Force

What is the ASVAB?

It's a test that is designed to measure your aptitude. The test includes a total combined ten tests to determine your skill level in:

- ➢ Word knowledge
- ➢ Reading comprehension
- ➢ Mathematics
- ➢ General science
- ➢ Arithmetic reasoning
- ➢ Automotive knowledge
- ➢ Mechanics
- ➢ Electronics
- ➢ Numerical operations
- ➢ Coding speed

You will receive individual scores in each of these areas but those scores are also combined to provide you with three unique scores:

- ➢ Math
- ➢ Verbal
- ➢ Academic

What to Know Before you Sign

I highly encourage you to take a practice test before applying to join the Air Force. That way, you will know where you stand and what areas you should improve upon.

How can I prepare for the Air Force?

Never stop learning and stay physically fit.

If you have yet to graduate high school then you should focus on your education above all else. Don't drop out of school. Don't do drugs and be sure not to get into any trouble.

Try to take more advanced classes like High Level English, Science, and Math. If possible, try and score some college credits since these will provide you with more opportunities later on – including a higher starting pay.

Exercise at least 3 days every week. Focus on running, pushups, and sit-ups.

Can I Join the Air Force if I have served in another branch of the military?

Yes, but the Air Force only accepts prior-service people on a limited basis.

Can I Join If I am Not a U.S. Citizen?

No. Only legal United States citizens are allowed to apply. You can apply as an immigrant if you have your green card.

Can I Apply if I Live in Another Country?

Yes, but you must use the online form to reach a local recruiter. You cannot sent an application through the mail from another country.

How Long is Air Force Basic Training?

Basic training is 8 ½ weeks.

What is Basic Training Like?

It's designed to be tough in order to bring out the full potential of each individual. Boot camp consists of intense physical training and rigid classroom study. It's not quite the "cussing and spitting" experience that many people portray it to be, but it is designed to be challenging. If it were easy, then everyone would do it!

Should I Prepare for Basic Training?

Of course! If you are fit when you arrive then you will have a much easier time. Focus on running, pushups, and sit-ups. Preparation is so important that I have devoted an entire chapter to helping you prepare for basic training. I will be blunt with you. If you are prepared then basic training will not be that difficult. If you are not prepared, then it's going to be hell.

What to Know Before you Sign

What is the Airman Education and Commissioning Program?

If you have already accumulated 45 semester hours from an accredited college then you are eligible for this program. However, there are a lot of applicants for this program. Those lucky enough to get selected are able to attend full-time college courses in areas that are deemed as the most critical.

Furthermore, all Airmen who are enrolled in this program receive an instant promotion to the rank of Staff Sergeant. They get the full pay and benefits that go along with that position.

What is Officer Training School?

Air Force Officer School is a program that teaches the fundamentals of leadership. Officer training instills professional ethics and evaluates the leadership potential of all those who are selected.

What are the qualifications for Officer Training School?

Generally speaking, an officer is required to graduate college prior to being commissioned. They are then trained by the Air Force to lead.

Officers don't exactly *enlist* in the Air Force. Instead, they apply for Officers Training School along with a lot of others. There is a lot of competition so your GPA will need to be extremely high to even be considered.

In order to quality for this process, you must:

➢ Be a legal citizen of the United States

➢ Pass Air Force Basic Training

➢ Take the AFOQT

➢ Score high on the SAT or the ACT.

➢ Have accumulated no less than 90 college credits

➢ Be between the ages of 18 and 35. Air Force Pilots must submit their applications before they are 28 -1/2 years old.

➢ Complete a physical examination within six months of submitting your application.

How do I become a pilot?

Pilots are officers who compete for pilot training slots. Pilots are trained by a special program called the Undergraduate Pilot Program.

Pilots require 20/50 vision while navigators require 20/200.

Is technical training different from boot camp?

Yes! Technical training is specifically catered to the specialty that you have applied to. It is more like a work detail where the overall focus is to train you in the specialty that you have selected.

Will I get paid while in basic training?

What to Know Before you Sign

Of course! You are paid every day that you serve. The amount you receive is based on your rank.

What questions should I ask my recruiter?

Recruiters are required to give you an accurate picture of what life in the service is like. Take advantage of this by asking questions. Here are some of the most important questions to ask your recruiter:

- ➤ What are the qualifications and details for my specialty?
- ➤ Where can I find videos that will teach me how to train in the Air Force?
- ➤ What is life in Boot Camp like?
- ➤ Are there any special enlistment programs available?
- ➤ Are there any guaranteed training programs available?

Joining the Air Force Comes with some Amazing Benefits!

While joining any branch of the United States military requires a lot of sacrifices, there are also a lot of benefits that are designed to repay you for those sacrifices.

Get a Steady Income: You are guaranteed to be paid on time, every time! All branches of the military pay on the 1st and 15th of every month. Your base pay is determined by your rank and job.

11 Simple Tools to Survive your First Year in the Air Force

Paid Vacations: You will earn two and a half days of paid vacation every month of services, which adds up to 30 days per year. You can accumulate up to 60 days of paid vacation time.

You will Get Specialized Training: You choose your Air Force career path based on your abilities so you are going to be trained in an area that you are qualified. Plus, you will get specialized training in this area.

Tax-Free Allowances: You can receive allowances for things like housing and subsistence if the government does not provide housing and food facilities where you are stationed. You will even get a uniform allowance to use for keeping your uniforms in tip-top shape.

Tax Advantage: You will only have to pay taxes on your base salary.

GI Bill: This bill pays for college and tuition for you and all direct family members. It's an amazing benefit.

Assistance with Tuition: You are allowed to continue your education while on active duty. The Air Force could help you with the cost of tuition of certain college courses.

Advancement is Based on your Skills: You are promoted by how well you perform, your knowledge, and other requirements.

What to Know Before you Sign

Health Care: All of your medical and dental care is covered while you are on active duty.

Life Insurance: Active duty military members can receive up to $200,000 in life insurance for a very low rate of $18 per month.

There's More!

You might even get allowances for commissions, temporary lodging, travel, and home loans designed specifically for veterans.

Chapter 2

Prepare for Basic Training

Studying in Advance

First of all, you are not required to study for anything in advance to graduate from basic training. By this point, you should have already graduated high school and passed your Armed Forces Vocational Aptitude Battery (ASVAB) test. That proves to your recruiter that you are smart enough to learn everything required to pass the mental part of basic training. Does that mean that you shouldn't worry about studying ahead of time? Not at all!

One of the first lessons that you're sure to learn during basic training is that there is not enough time to do everything that you had expected going in. Time is a commodity that you're not going to have in abundance. There are no exceptions to this rule. By studying ahead of time, you will be gaining a step on your training. In other words, the more time you spend studying before basic training, the less time you will have to study during this tough time. That will free up time to get some of those other hundreds of tasks done and might just keep that big, scary man out of your face for a few minutes. Okay, probably not but at least you won't be stressing as much over passing classroom tests.

Prepare for Basic Training

Here are a few areas that you can study in advance of basic training. It might not seem like much but just a little bit of preparation can go a long way.

Air Force Ranks

There are two types of ranking structures in the Air Force. Learn both before leaving for basic training:

Enlisted: This rank is expressed by stripes. Higher ranking personnel have more stripes.

Officers: An Officer's ranking is expressed as bars, leafs, and stars. The lowest ranking Officer outranks the highest ranking enlisted Airman.

One of the requirements of graduating is that you memorize every rank in the Air Force. This is something that you can get done right now.

Learn Military Time

This is probably one of the easiest preparations for basic training. Most of us already know how *military time* works but I recommend that you start making this transition the moment you sign with your recruiter. Change your clocks to military time. Stop using AM and PM, even in your normal life. If you see a clock that reads 2PM, in your mind it should read as 1400 hours.

Military Time at a Glance

Standard Time	Military Time	Standard Time	Military Time
12:00 AM	0000 Hours	12:00 PM	1200 Hours
1:00 AM	0100 Hours	1:00 PM	1300 Hours
2:00 AM	0200 Hours	2:00 PM	1400 Hours
3:00 AM	0300 Hours	3:00 PM	1500 Hours
4:00 AM	0400 Hours	4:00 PM	1600 Hours
5:00 AM	0500 Hours	5:00 PM	1700 Hours
6:00 AM	0600 Hours	6:00 PM	1800 Hours
7:00 AM	0700 Hours	7:00 PM	1900 Hours
8:00 AM	0800 Hours	8:00 PM	2000 Hours
9:00 AM	0900 Hours	9:00 PM	2100 Hours
10:00 AM	1000 Hours	10:00 PM	2200 Hours
11:00 AM	1100 Hours	11:00 PM	2300 Hours

Prepare for Basic Training

➤ Most things military related use local time for whatever area you are stationed in.

➤ Military observes Daylight Savings Time if it is recognized in the area where you're stationed.

Greenwich Mean Time (GMT)

If two Air Force bases located in different time zones are coordinating with each other, then they use the globally recognized time in Greenwich, England in order to avoid confusion. This is known as GMT, but in military terms it's called "Zulu". If you hear "Zulu" suffixed to a time, then the time is being given as GMT.

Learn the Phonetic Alphabet

A Phonetic alphabet is a list of words that are used to communicate letters when sending a message by radio or over a telephone. By speaking words you are able to avoid mistakes with letters that sound similar like "M" and "N". For example, you would spell Air Force as follows:

Alpha

India

Romeo

Foxtrot

Oscar

Romeo

Charlie

Echo

Military Phonetic Alphabet at a Glance

A	Alpha		N	November
B	Bravo		O	Oscar
C	Charlie		P	Papa
D	Delta		Q	Quebec
E	Echo		R	Romeo
F	Foxtrot		S	Sierra
G	Golf		T	Tango
H	Hotel		U	Uniform
I	India		V	Victor
J	Juliette		W	Whisky
K	Kilo		X	X-Ray
L	Lima		Y	Yankee
M	Mike		Z	Zulu

Prepare for Basic Training

Memorize your Social Security Number

You will be using this number for almost everything since it becomes your identification number. Go ahead and memorize it if you haven't done so already.

Practice Drill

Drill is when military personnel march in unison. They step, turn, start, and stop in unison. However, drill is not limited to just marching. It can be just learning to stand in unison in a disciplined way.

You can count on the fact that you're going to be doing a lot of drill during basic training. In fact, during the first two weeks you're going to be spending a couple of hours per day on this. If you start practicing drill before you step foot into basic training then your life is going to be a lot easier. I recommend that you practice properly saluting at the very least.

Learn your Chain of Command

Businesses have a corporate ladder – the Air Force has a Chain of Command. While the civilian world does enforce this ladder for managing most businesses, you will find that the Air Force emphasizes this chain much more prominently than you're used to.

In the military, you better not try and go above your commander's head if you have a problem. The correct

method is to report problems to the appropriate person –
who will be the lowest level in your Chain of Command. Then
if that person cannot help, you can move up to the next level.
With that said, the Air Force is going to require you to
memorize your entire Chain of Command during the first
week of basic training. Why not go ahead and learn it in
advance?

Learn the Air Force Song
Every branch of the military has its own specific song. They
are all proud of it. You can count on the fact that you will be
singing this song at least once every day. I recommend that
you go ahead and learn the lyrics.

Core Values
Each branch of the military also has its own set of core
values. These are standards that every member is expected
to live by. You are going to be required to memorize these
core values and recite them anytime that you are ordered.
Go ahead and learn then before you begin basic training.

Getting in Shape
During your Air Force Basic Training, you will be required to
pass a physical fitness test before you can graduate. You are
going to be physically trained six days per week but there are
some minimum fitness standards that the Air Force
recommends for all new recruits. You should try and meet
these standards before you arrive at basic training:

Recommended Physical Fitness Level

Men

1.5 Mile Run: 14 Minutes

2 Mile Run: 19 Minutes

Pushups: 34

Sit-Ups: 38

Women

1.5 Mile Run: 16 Minutes

2 Mile Run: 23 Minutes

Pushups: 21

Sit-Ups: 38

Keep in mind that the numbers above are not the standards required for graduation. They are minimum recommendations that you should meet before you start basic training. You will find that basic training will be much more difficult if you are not able to meet these standards when starting.

When you arrive at basic training, you are going to be required to undergo an initial fitness text. If you do not meet the minimum recommendations then you are going to get the attention of your T.I. – which is always unwanted. Plus, you will be required to dedicate even more time to physical training!

Note: It's also worth noting that if your performance is exemplary during this initial test then you will also get the unwanted attention of your T.I. I recommend that you try and perform average during this initial test, even if you are capable of performing at an extremely high level.

Now most of those exercising for basic training make a huge mistake – they train themselves to become victims rather than truly preparing. Here's what I mean.

Half-effort pushups are not going to be tolerated. They must be performed using a perfect form.

How to Do Pushups the Right Way
Align your arms with your shoulders and keep your feet no more than 12 inches apart. Your body must form a straight line from your shoulders to your ankles. Keep your head up, lower your body, and then push back up.

Note: If your feet are further than 12 inches apart or your body is not straight then the pushup will not count.

How to Do Sit-Ups the Right Way
Lay flat on your back and align your feet with your body so they are no more than 12 inches apart. Bend your knees square with your body with a spotter holding your feet. Cross your arms over your chest, placing each hand on the

opposite shoulder. Pull your body forward until your elbows touch your knees, then slowly lower until your shoulders touch the ground.

Note: If you do not physically touch your knees with your elbows then the sit-up will not count. If you put your hands behind your head then it will not count.

How to Training at Running

Running for long distances is an area where many people struggle. Start out by running at a slow pace for at least 15 minutes a day and then increase it by 1 minute each day until you are running for 40 minutes continuously. You should run at least 5 times per week.

Easy to Follow Workout Plan

Basic training is designed to ensure that you are physically and mentally fit. It's not a rite of passage torture session that you're put through for their amusement. With that said, you should prepare yourself for the rigors of basic training by following this workout plan.

The Air Force recommends that you begin physically training six weeks before basic training but I believe that you should start two-three months ahead of time. After all, being physically fit will not only prepare you to basic training but it will make you feel great! Exercise at least 5 times per week and follow these guidelines with each workout.

11 Simple Tools to Survive your First Year in the Air Force

Week 1

- ➢ **Stretch**: 5 Minutes
- ➢ **Rapidly Rotate Between Sit-Ups and Pushups**: 2 Minutes.
- ➢ **Walk:** 5 Minutes
- ➢ **Jog:** 1 Minute
- ➢ **Walk:** 5 Minutes
- ➢ **Jog:** 1 Minute
- ➢ **Walk:** 5 Minutes
- ➢ **Stretch:** 2 Minutes

Week 2

- ➢ **Stretch:** 5 Minutes
- ➢ **Rapidly Rotate Between Sit-Ups and Pushups:** 2 Minutes.
- ➢ **Walk:** 5 Minutes
- ➢ **Jog:** 3 Minutes
- ➢ **Walk:** 5 Minutes
- ➢ **Jog:** 3 Minute
- ➢ **Walk:** 5 Minutes
- ➢ **Stretch:** 2 Minutes

Prepare for Basic Training

Week 3

- ➤ **Stretch:** 5 Minutes
- ➤ **Rapidly Rotate Between Sit-Ups and Pushups:** 2 Minutes.
- ➤ **Walk:** 4 Minutes
- ➤ **Jog:** 5 Minutes
- ➤ **Walk:** 4 Minutes
- ➤ **Jog:** 5Minute
- ➤ **Walk:** 5 Minutes
- ➤ **Stretch:** 2 Minutes

Week 4

- ➤ **Stretch:** 5 Minutes
- ➤ **Rapidly Rotate Between Sit-Ups and Pushups:** 4 Minutes.
- ➤ **Walk:** 4 Minutes
- ➤ **Jog:** 5 Minutes
- ➤ **Walk:** 4 Minutes
- ➤ **Jog:** 5 Minutes
- ➤ **Walk:** 5 Minutes
- ➤ **Stretch:** 2 Minutes

Week 5

- ➢ **Stretch:** 5 Minutes
- ➢ **Rapidly Rotate Between Sit-Ups and Pushups:** 4 Minutes.
- ➢ **Walk:** 4 Minutes
- ➢ **Jog:** 6 Minutes
- ➢ **Walk:** 4 Minutes
- ➢ **Jog:** 6 Minutes
- ➢ **Walk:** 5 Minutes
- ➢ **Stretch:** 2 Minutes

Week 6

- ➢ **Stretch:** 5 Minutes
- ➢ **Rapidly Rotate Between Sit-Ups and Pushups:** 4 Minutes.
- ➢ **Walk:** 4 Minutes
- ➢ **Jog:** 7 Minutes
- ➢ **Walk:** 4 Minutes
- ➢ **Jog:** 7 Minutes
- ➢ **Walk:** 5 Minutes
- ➢ **Stretch:** 2 Minutes

Prepare for Basic Training

Week 7

➢ **Stretch:** 5 Minutes

➢ **Rapidly Rotate Between Sit-Ups and Pushups:** 6 Minutes.

➢ **Walk:** 4 Minutes

➢ **Jog:** 8 Minutes

➢ **Walk:** 4 Minutes

➢ **Jog:** 8 Minutes

➢ **Walk:** 5 Minutes

➢ **Stretch:** 2 Minutes

Week 8

➢ **Stretch:** 5 Minutes

➢ **Rapidly Rotate Between Sit-Ups and Pushups:** 6 Minutes.

➢ **Walk:** 4 Minutes

➢ **Jog:** 9 Minutes

➢ **Walk:** 4 Minutes

➢ **Jog:** 9 Minutes

➢ **Walk:** 5 Minutes

➢ **Stretch:** 2 Minutes

11 Simple Tools to Survive your First Year in the Air Force

Week 9

- ➢ Stretch: 5 Minutes
- ➢ **Rapidly Rotate Between Sit-Ups and Pushups:** 4 Minutes.
- ➢ **Walk:** 4 Minutes
- ➢ **Run:** 13 Minutes
- ➢ **Walk:** 5 Minutes
- ➢ **Stretch:** 2 Minutes

Week 10

- ➢ **Stretch:** 5 Minutes
- ➢ **Rapidly Rotate Between Sit-Ups and Pushups:** 4 Minutes.
- ➢ **Walk:** 4 Minutes
- ➢ **Run:** 15 Minutes
- ➢ **Walk:** 5 Minutes
- ➢ **Stretch:** 2 Minutes

Week 11

- ➢ **Stretch:** 5 Minutes
- ➢ **Rapidly Rotate Between Sit-Ups and Pushups:** 2 Minutes.
- ➢ **Walk:** 4 Minutes

Prepare for Basic Training

- ➢ **Run:** 17 Minutes
- ➢ **Walk:** 5 Minutes
- ➢ **Stretch:** 2 Minutes

Week 12

- ➢ **Stretch:** 5 Minutes
- ➢ **Rapidly Rotate Between Sit-Ups and Pushups:** 2 Minutes.
- ➢ **Walk:** 1 Minutes
- ➢ **Run:** 17 Minutes
- ➢ **Walk:** 5 Minutes
- ➢ **Stretch:** 2 Minutes

Week 13

- ➢ **Stretch:** 5 Minutes
- ➢ **Rapidly Rotate Between Sit-Ups and Pushups:** 2 Minutes.
- ➢ **Walk:** 2 Minutes
- ➢ **Jog:** 2 Minutes
- ➢ **Run:** 17 Minutes
- ➢ **Walk:** 5 Minutes
- ➢ **Stretch:** 2 Minutes

Week 14

> ➤ Stretch. 5 Minutes

> ➤ **Rapidly Rotate Between Sit-Ups and Pushups:** 2 Minutes.

> ➤ **Jog:** 3 Minutes

> ➤ **Run:** 17 Minutes

> ➤ **Walk:** 5 Minutes

> ➤ **Stretch:** 2 Minutes

Developing a physical routine will not only get you into shape but it will teach you how to follow routines, which are a normal part of military life.

Things to Tell Your Family

Your parents are going to worry about you while you're off at basic training so give them a bit of assurance by providing them with some vital information. Sit down and tell them everything that you know about what to expect. Let's look at some of the more important areas of concern now.

What to Do In Case of a Family Emergency

Remind your family that you cannot receive phone calls during basic training, even if there's a family emergency. So what can your family do if there's an emergency?

An emergency must first be certified through the American

Prepare for Basic Training

Red Cross. Let your family know that if there is an emergency that they must contact the American Red Cross. Also, they can only attempt to contact you if it's a real emergency like death or a serious illness in the family. They will need to provide:

> ➢ Your Full Name

> ➢ Your Social Security Number

> ➢ Your Flight Address (if they have not received the flight address yet, then the Red Cross can still find you.)

Mail Call

Once you have been at basic training for around a week or so, you will be allowed to mail a postcard home. This postcard will have your flight address on it. Since you can only send this to one person, make sure that person knows how to get in touch with all of your friends and other family members.

Let your family know that you are not going to have a lot of time during basic training so you will not be able to send out very many letters. In fact, you should plan on the fact that you will only be able to send out two very short letters during your whole stay at basic training. That doesn't mean that your family shouldn't write you though! It's important that they write you as often as they can. Basic training can get lonely and is emotionally exhausting. A cheerful letter from home might make all of the difference in the world.

Make sure that your family knows that they should never send you any gifts. Sure, they will allow them to pass through but then your T.I. will just shout at you and then throw it away.

Mail call happens at the same time for everyone so keep in mind that the T.I. will read anything aloud that is disclosed on the outside of the envelope. Therefore, your family should keep all information inside of the envelope.

Phone Call Policy
Make sure that your family understands the Air Force phone call policy. You're going to be permitted one call early in basic training. During that time, you're going to be under a great deal of stress and might sound exhausted or even scared. It's perfectly normal so prepare them for it before leaving.

Prepare Them for Graduation
Inform your family that they will receive an invitation to attend your graduation. That invitation will give them all of the details that they will need in order to attend. It's an experience that they will never forget so encourage them to attend!

Prepare for Basic Training

Pack Light

An often overlooked preparation is packing for your stay at basic training. Your recruiter will give you a list of what's allowed. If it is not on that list, then you better not take it. It's amazing at how many people think that certain items will be an exception. Trust me, there are no exceptions. That list has been around for a long time.

One of the first experiences you will have at basic training is your items being searched. Anything that is not approved will be taken away. In fact, you should probably forget about bringing most items on that list anyway and here's why.

Training Instructors absolutely love it when everyone conforms to the same look. They will pick on anyone who dresses differently or uses a product that is different. When you arrive at basic training, you are taken to a troop mall where you are allowed to purchase everything you need for basic training. If you are using this stuff, your T.I. is going to like you a lot better!

Plus, T.I.s love to play games with new recruits and these games mostly involve your luggage. Packing light will make these games much easier. When asked if they would change anything about their preparation for basic training, most cadets say that they wish they had packed less!

With that in mind, here are some items that I recommend you pack:

- ➤ **Driver's License.** Even though you're not going to be driving while at basic training, some jobs in the Air Force require you to have a driver's license. You have to be able to prove that you have one in order to be eligible for those jobs.

- ➤ **Social Security Card.**

- ➤ **College transcripts, Civil Air Patrol Certificates, and any JROTC Certificates.** You will not actually need these during basic training but you want them for your final trip. Having these items will give you college credits that allow you to get an immediate advanced enlistment ranking.

- ➤ **Marriage License and Birth Certificates for Dependents**. You will need these in order to start a housing allowance, family separation allowance, or to apply for dependent ID cards.

- ➤ **Banking Information.** More specifically, the name of your bank, routing number, and account number. A blank check will work but you can also bring a blank deposit slip. The military requires that your pay is directly deposited into your bank account.

- ➤ **Debit/ATM Card.**

- ➤ **Limited Amount of Cash.** Bring as few bills as possible and limit it to no more than $50. You will be allowed to keep cash in your personal security drawer but you have to record the serial number for all bills in a notebook. That list must always be kept up-to-date.

➢ **Prescriptions.** You cannot bring any medication with you. If you are required to take a prescription medication, the military doctor will prescribe it to you and it must be picked up at a military pharmacy. Over-the-counter medication is not allowed during basic training.

➢ **Dental Care Items.** Your toothbrush tray must be the square kind. The round kind will roll out of place when the drawer is opened and your T.I. will not be happy. Toothpaste should be equipped with a flip-top lid. The screw lid will be impossible to keep clean.

➢ **Shampoo.** You need to bring the square bottle type of shampoo because the round bottle will roll around on inspection.

➢ **Soap.** Liquid soap is the best because it's easy to keep *"inspection ready."*

➢ **Deodorant**

➢ **Black Ball-Point Pen.** Even though the official list tells you that blue is acceptable, the Air Force prefers black ink.

➢ **Notebook.** Only pack a small notebook since you can purchase one a few days into basic training. It's used to take notes until you get to the mall.

➢ **Shaving Essentials.** You are "allowed" to bring an electric razor but those are so difficult to keep clean that you should stick to a standard razor for basic training.

➢ **Civilian Clothes for Four Days.** You will be issued uniforms on the fourth day of basic training. This includes underwear. The only exception is that women get to purchase underwear at the BX since there are too many shapes and sizes to issue them.

➢ **Civilian Eyeglasses.** Only if you require them to see. You will be assigned military glasses after about two weeks of basic training.

➢ **Pre-Stamped Envelopes.** So you never have to worry about running out of stamps.

➢ **Brush or Comb.** This is only applicable for women. Men will not have any hair left to comb by the second day of basic training.

➢ **Watch.** You are allowed to wear a watch during basic training so long as it's conservative. It's a handy item to have.

Packing Tips

Take care when you are packing for the Air Force. Remember those fun games I mentioned that T.I.s love to play on new recruits? These games will start when they dump your whole bag out in front of everyone. Then he/she will start to poke

Prepare for Basic Training

fun of anything that looks unusual. Even a book will be the subject of criticism!

Pack only clothes that have no writing, slogans, or pictures on them. If you do, then you can be assured that your first day is going to be memorable – and not in a good way.

Keeping all of that in mind, I will leave you with two important things to remember:

1. Anything that you bring will have to be kept spotlessly clean all of the time. Bring only items that are easy to clean.

2. Everything you need will be issued to you by the Air Force. This includes uniforms, flashlights, etc. You will also be taken to the BX and told what else you should purchase.

When you arrive at boot camp, you are issued a debit card that has $300 for these purchases. This amount is taken out of your first paycheck. Think ahead as you pack and consider that everything you do while at basic training is under scrutiny.

Chapter 3

How to Survive Basic Training

How You Will Get There

Air Force Basic Training takes place at the Lackland Air Force Basic Military Training facility. Most cadets will use commercial travel to reach Lackland. You might find yourself flying with another group from your local processing station. Your destination will be the San Antonio airport, where you will then report to Terminal A, the Air Force Receiving Station.

Upon arrival, you will be greeted by a few Training Instructors (T.I.) who will verify your orders and the direct you to the waiting area. At this point, the T.I.s will be very friendly but make no mistake that the discipline will begin as soon as you're on the bus. After all, military discipline is always done behind closed doors!

You might have to wait a long time on the bus but you should enjoy this relaxation while it lasts. Chat with others and get to know your fellow cadets.

Your first stop will be the Welcome Center. This is where you turn in your records and get a little bit of preliminary processing out of the way. Once that's over, you will be taken to the dormitory. Never call it "barracks." If you do, then your Air Force T.I. will remind you that there are no "barracks" on an Air Force base. We will discuss this in more detail before long so be patient.

The T.I.s on the bus are friendly enough, although you are likely to see a much stricter side than at the airport. However, once you step off the bus then it all changes.

Meeting your T.I.

You will meet your new training team as soon as you step off the bus. This team will be led by a Chief Military Training Instructor, called your T.I. by only their friends and family. You will address them as "sir" or "ma'am" at all times. It's at this moment when all hell breaks loose and you know that you have gotten yourself into a tough situation!

Your flight (Air Force term for platoon) will have no less than a T.I. and an Assistant T.I. Sometimes there might be more than that but you should hope that it's just the two.

In the Air Force, you are required to address all noncommissioned officers (NCOs) as "Sir" or "Ma'am." However, once you graduate from basic training then you can break from that routine. In fact, I'm sure you will slip up and call one of your instructors "Sir" or "Ma'am" and get scolded for your good manners. Anyways, let's get back on topic here.

Preparation to Meet your T.I. Begins At Home

Yes, you read that correctly. You need to prepare for this meeting before you even step foot out of your house. You do not want your personal appearance to cause you to stand out. Trust me, there are going to be a few who do and when you see what happens to them, you'll be glad that you are not one of them!

> ➢ Cut your hair (men).

> ➢ Women should be sure that they keep their hair off of their shirt collar. I encourage you to just cut your hair so that it's short enough to not have to be put up. Hair grows back.

> ➢ Do not wear earrings or other jewelry.

> ➢ Shave.

> ➢ Wear clothes that fit you.

Training Instructors will not cuss at you; nor will they put their hands on you (unless you attack them, which would be very stupid). However, they have crafted the art of yelling! They can make you feel six inches tall without using a single cuss word.

Another thing that you will quickly learn is that no matter how much you prepare, you're not going to do anything right. You will stand wrong, walk wrong, even your breathing will be wrong! That's why you would rather the T.I. be focusing their yelling at the unprepared guy who showed up for basic training with long hair. However, under no circumstances should you giggle or smile at the expense of another cadet. Doing so will shift attention to you, which if you haven't figured out is something you always try to avoid.

➤ Never use the words yeah, nope, uh-huh, or anything lazy.

➤ Always begin **or** end all sentences with the word "sir" or "ma'am". Most T.I.s do not like you to use a "sir sandwich" which means beginning and ending a sentence with "sir."

➤ You'll never be able to speak loud enough.

➤ T.I.s will assume that you're deaf and yell right next to your ear. Even so, never show any signs of discomfort or else you will get rewarded with – you guessed it – more yelling!

It won't take long for you to realize that your Training Instructor doesn't care that you have a first name. Don't worry, he/she doesn't care if the person standing next to you has a name either. You can expect to either be called "trainee" or "recruit."

You can expect to get welcomed to basic training by playing some of the T.I.s favorite games. Here are a few.

T.I. Have Certain Games that They Love to Play

Normally, you arrive at basic training during the evening or at night. Therefore, your first day won't last very long. However, that doesn't mean that the T.I. isn't going to have a little fun with you before lights out so you're probably going to be introduced to one of the following games.

The Fire Drill

Fire drill is a T.I. favorite and it will quickly make you appreciate having packed lightly (hopefully you follow my advice). You have to carry your bags from the drill pad to your bunk as quickly as possible. After which, you carry your bags back to the drill pad again and line up in formation. Make sure that you line up in the same order as you were when you left.

Pick 'em Up / Put 'em Down

According to new recruits, this game seems to have slowly replaced Fire Drill as a T.I. favorite. In fact, you might get to play this game from the time you arrive at basic training until lights out. The name says it all; you pick up your bags and put them down as quickly as possible.

Report to Me!

Everyone is required to hold their bag while standing in formation until everyone gives their reporting statement. Again, if you packed light then this is not that difficult. On the other hand, if you packed heavily then you're going to regret it!

How to Survive Basic Training

A Typical Day in Basic Training

First of all, let me inform you that there really is no "typical day" at basic training. Every day is going to be different. You'll get to experience a lot of new activities every day. With that said, the Air Force does love procedure so you can expect all of your days to look something like this:

0445: Reveille. Wake Up Call.

0500: Get into formation and ready for PC.

0500-0600: Physical Conditioning. You will alternate daily between running and aerobics.

0600-0615: Breakfast. You will have to eat fast!

0630-0745: Get the Dorm in Tip Top Shape.

0800-1130: This time is reserved for whatever your T.I. sees fit. It could be used for records checks, classes, drilling, or even shots.

1130-1230: Lunch Time.

1300-1700: This time is normally reserved for the classroom, especially during the summer.

1700-1800: Dinner. This time will vary depending on how long you have been at basic training.

1900-2045: Nighttime Dorm Setup. Clean up, shine your boots, and sometimes you might even get a patio break.

2100: Lights Out.

Physical Fitness Training

Physical Fitness of new cadets was emphasized more by the Air Force, starting in 2003. Now all entrants must undergo a preliminary physical fitness test when they first enter basic training. They must also pass a final fitness test in order to graduate. Therefore, you can expect to be exercising – a lot! In fact, you will be training six days per week. This training includes three days of aerobic running and three days of muscular endurance training.

Physical fitness training always begins with a 15-20 minute stretch session.

Running sessions are divided into 40 minute group sessions, self-paced running, and 30 second sprints that are separated by brisk walking sessions.

You can expect to be timed on a two mile run every week. If you don't perform as expected then you will get some unwanted attention from your T.I.

Muscular endurance training alternates between the following exercises during the course of 48 minutes:

➢ Crunches

➢ Leg lifts

➢ Pushups

➢ Sit-Ups

How to Survive Basic Training

➢ Flutter Kicks

➢ Pull-Ups

This process is designed for the sole purpose of improving your strength.

What to Expect if you Get Disciplined

You will get a lovely explanation of the discipline process on your first day at basic training. Recruits are given several tiny forms that are famously known as 341s. When you screw up, your T.I. will remove one of these forms. If you get too many of them pulled, then they will *recycle* you. Trust me when I say that you do not want to be recycled.

Every day of basic training is registered as its own individual day. For example, you will have Day One, Day Two, Day Three, Day Four – I think you get the point. Let's assume that you have made it all the way up to Day Thirty of basic training. Your squadron commander can *recycle* you back down to Day Seven, where you will be placed in a new flight. There, you can be assured that you will have the full attention of the T.I. The objective is that you are given the opportunity to relearn what you failed to learn in the first place.

Recycling is the ultimate threat and it's used to keep everyone motivated. However, it's not as easy to recycle as your T.I. might want you to believe. The truth is that you have to be a real *screw-up* in order to be recycled. You'll be able to spot the ones who will get recycled almost immediately. So don't be too afraid of this.

Most infractions, so long as they are minor, are disciplined by straight up *"dropping you"* for pushups. There are regulations in place that restrict the number of pushups that a T.I. can force but he/she can *"drop"* you five times in a row! Plus, this is where a T.I.s *"bad hearing"* might become a factor. They won't hear your count and you will have to start over. Plus, they can always make you do a slow count, holding you in the down position for a long period of time.

That last paragraph was for those of you who might be tempted to become a *"dormitory lawyer"* by informing your T.I. that he/she "cannot force you to do that."

Finally, we will move onto the worst form of punishment, **"Correctional Custody."** This form of discipline is reserved for those who have a serious attitude problem. You do not want to get put into CC. The only thing worse than CC is being discharged. Correctional Custody is much tougher than basic training. Every single step you take through the day is controlled. Again, don't try and be a "dormitory lawyer" or you could wind up in CC.

How Cadets in Basic Training get Paid
You will want to know that you're being paid for all of that hard work you're going through while at basic training. First of all, all US military pay requires the use of direct deposit. There are two options:

How to Survive Basic Training

I recommend that you set up a bank account before you leave for basic training. If you do, then you will need to provide them with your account information. Be sure to bring your debit card with you.

If you don't have a bank account (or forget to bring vital information) then the Air Force staff is going to make you establish an account at the base credit union.

Either way, when you are being processed, you will complete all paperwork to start getting paid. The military pays on the first and fifteenth of every month, unless the day falls on a non-duty day. In that case, you're paid on the first duty day that precedes the first or fifteenth.

When Can you Expect your First Paycheck?
This is a question that is really tough to answer because there are so many variables, but I will try to the best of my ability.

If your information is put into the system before the sixth or seventh of the month, then you can expect to receive your first paycheck on the fifteenth.

If the information is input between the seventh and twenty-third, then you won't receive your first paycheck until the first of the following month.

Note: Your information is not entered into the system on the same day that you fill out the paperwork. The financial clerk is entering hundreds of other recruits into the system so it can take several days to get your information entered into the system.

The rule of thumb is to never expect your first paycheck until 30 days after you fill out the application – just to be safe.

If you are worried about not getting paid for your first week or two at basic training then here's some great news. No matter when you get your first paycheck, you're going to receive any back pay that is due to you.

Enlisting with an advanced rank will allow you to start basic receiving the full pay for that rank, even though you're not officially ranked until after graduation.

You Get a Basic Training Debit Card
You will get everything that you need for basic training issued to you during basic training. However, it's not given to you for free. Only your uniform will be free but anything that is not related to your uniform will come at your expense. This includes items like pens, notebooks, and flashlights.

Not to worry though because you're going to be issued a basic training debit card that comes loaded with $300, which is deducted from your first paycheck. You can use this card to make purchases that are not issued for free. If there are funds left on this card when you're finished with basic training then it will be added to your paycheck.

How to Survive Basic Training

Cash

You can have a limited amount of cash for use during patio breaks but the amount you can have is determined by your T.I. However, all cash must be locked away in your security drawer and you have to keep track of the serial number of every bill in a pocket notebook. It will be checked so make sure that you keep this journal up to date. You will need cash to purchase sodas and snacks while on your patio break.

You Must Pass a Final Fitness Test to Graduate

You are required to pass a physical fitness test in order to graduate from Air Force Basic Training. This test includes a timed run, pushups, and sit-ups. Pull-ups are for those who are looking for a fitness award. However, pull-ups are not required in order to graduate.

I told you earlier that you should prepare for this before your departure but by this point, basic training will have you in shape to be able to meet the minimum graduation requirements.

These standards are just for passing basic training. Depending on your department in the Air Force, you will be required to maintain a certain level of fitness. Those who are able to meet the requirements of an honor graduate are given special awards. If you can achieve the Warhawk status, then you are given a t-shirt, certificate, and you get an extra day pass off-base during graduation.

What Happens if you Fail?

If you happen to fail the Physical Training evaluation then not all is lost. You're not going to be immediately discharged. Instead, you will be recycled a couple of weeks to another flight where you are given more time to get into shape.

If you were really close to meeting the standards then you will likely be given another chance to pass on the following day.

PT Requirements for Graduation

Male Minimum Fitness Requirements

Run (1.5 Miles): 11:57

Push-Ups (1 Minute): 33

Sit-Ups (1 Minute): 42

Female Minimum Fitness Requirements

Run (1.5 Miles): 14:26

Push-Ups (1 Minute): 18

Sit-Ups (1 Minute): 38

How to Survive Basic Training

Male Thunderbolt Fitness Requirements

Run (1.5 Miles): 9:30

Push-Ups (1 Minute): 55

Sit-Ups (1 Minute): 60

Pull-Ups: 5

Female Thunderbolt Fitness Requirements

Run (1.5 Miles): 12:00

Push-Ups (1 Minute): 32

Sit-Ups (1 Minute): 55

Pull-Ups: 2

Male Warhawk Fitness Requirements

Run (1.5 Miles): 8:55

Push-Ups (1 Minute): 65

Sit-Ups (1 Minute): 70

Pull-Ups: 10

Female Warhawk Fitness Requirements

Run (1.5 Miles): 10:55

Push-Ups (1 Minute): 40

Sit-Ups (1 Minute): 60

Pull-Ups: 5

Final Written Tests

Air Force graduates are also required to pass a written test before they can graduate. These tests include several written tests and quizzes but the final two are the most pivotal. Each text you are given consists of 100 questions. You must score a minimum of 70 percent to graduate. However, if you want to qualify as an honor graduate, then you are required to score over 90 percent.

Chapter 4

The Air Force EPR System

The Air Force has recently made some changes to the way it evaluates and promotes Airmen. Airmen who are looking to advance their careers are going through a major transition. What does this mean for you as a new recruit? This chapter is going to show you how this new system works.

The Air Force has been preparing this new EPR system for years and has even used feedback from airmen to help create it. So if you have been researching the Air Force promotion system prior to reading this book, then information you've found might be out of date. Let's take a look at a few of the notable changes.

The Five-Point Numerical System is Gone!

This is one of the first changes that the Air Force has made to the enlisted performance report. In the past, a five point numerical system was used to create EPR scores. However, this system quickly became inflated to the point where most airmen received what is known as a "firewall 5" out of the five points that are possible. The score essentially became useless.

That obsolete system is gone. Now, supervisors will begin assessing performance of airmen by selecting the response that best describes the airman's performance from a prewritten list. When it comes time for a promotion, commanders will then select eligible airmen's EPRs and put them into no less than four categories, starting with airmen who are most highly recommended for promotion. The bottom line is that only a small percentage of airmen will be recommended. This new quota is designed to limit the number of top recommendations, thus preventing the firewall 5 effect.

While this new system does bring up a lot of interesting questions and concerns from currently enrolled airmen, here's the bottom line.

This new quota is designed to determine which airmen have the greatest potential for promotion. Every squadron commander will select their top performers. Simply put, if you perform exceptionally at your job then you should be eligible for promotion.

Test Scores Count

Another major change that has been made is that testing is now an essential part of promotions. This includes both specialty tests and fitness examinations. In fact, this new system is a first for the Air Force.

As an Airman, you must score at least 40 for every test and their combined total must be at least 90. So if you want to be eligible for promotion then you have to score at least 90 combined points on the SKT and PFE tests.

The Air Force EPR System

Note: Airmen who only take the PFE test will have their test score doubled. Therefore, they must score at least 45.

Will This New System Lead to Favoritism?

There has been a lot of concern from current airmen that this new system will lead to favoritism. However, the new process is so transparent that it will be extremely difficult for supervisors to show favoritism. The supervisor will meet with each airman and they will go through a very detailed conversation about what is expected from them. Therefore, an airman shouldn't be surprised at their evaluation since their goals were set at the beginning of the year.

Since this feedback is visible to everyone in the supervisor's Chain of Command, there is a traceable trail to follow should a concern arise. This system is directly linked to performance. It would be extremely difficult for a supervisor to show this type of favoritism.

If that's not assurance enough, then a supervisor is also required to document negative evaluations.

Is Volunteering Still Important?

Simply put, yes. However, in the past some airmen could get promotions because they were heavy volunteers, even though they might struggle with their primary duties. That is now a thing of the past. Performance comes first, just as it should. However, it's being stressed that volunteering is still an important part of being a well-rounded airman.

The bottom line is that if you do not perform well at your primary job, then you're not going to be eligible for promotion. If you do perform at a high level, then volunteering will benefit that performance. The overall goal for the Air Force seems to be ensuring that performance is the most pivotal aspect of promotions.

Other Changes

 ➤ In the past, the Air Force has used the previous five EPRs for promotions up to technical sergeant. Now it has been changed to three.

 ➤ The maximum for weighed EPR points has been increased to 250. It used to be 135 points.

Chapter 5

Surviving Tests

Testing can be a daunting task by itself but when combined with all of the responsibilities that come with being an active Airman, it can become downright overwhelming! The key is to make things as easy as possible. This is done by developing successful study habits that help make these tests as easy as possible. This chapter is going to be devoted to showing you how to ace those tests. Preparation builds confidence which makes exams much less stressful.

Start by Developing Better Study Skills
By the time you are preparing for your first test, you should have already learned the power of routine. After all, routine is stressed repeatedly throughout all of basic training and routine will be stressed your entire career. This is a great habit since developing a study routine is going to make preparation a breeze.

First, you will need to determine what time of day is your most effective study time. Some of us study better in the morning while others are much more efficient at night.

Set a Schedule and Stick to It
Schedule the amount of time that you plan on studying, setting breaks at normal intervals. As you develop this

routine, slowly reduce the time of breaks between study sessions. Here's a quick look at an example:

Week 1: Study for 15 minutes and break for 10 minutes.

Week 2: Study for 20 minutes and break for 10 minutes.

Week 3: Study for 20 minutes and break for 5 minutes.

Week 4: Study for 30 minutes and break for 5 minutes.

Week 4 is your overall goal so once you have reached this level of study, stick with it.

Warm Up Before Each Study Session

Just like you stretch before physical training, you need to warm up your brain before you begin studying. Start each study session with a quick review of everything that you studied during the last session. The goal is to prepare and build confidence before you dive into the books.

Do this by creating a concept map so that you have an easy way to review your previous study session.

Join a Study Group

Study groups are helpful at keeping you motivated. It keeps study from becoming repetitive and boring. However, you should develop a list of guidelines to follow while working in groups. Make sure that the group you join is using the time efficiently.

Surviving Tests

Small study groups of three to four people seem to be the most effective. Each session should start with a review of information that was learned during the previous session.

Practice tests are also a good idea, especially for classes where information is cumulative.

Chart Study Records

There are so many different methods of studying that it's sometimes difficult to discover which one works best for you. Creating study charts in the beginning is a great way to eliminate this problem. This does not have to be a reoccurring tactic. Just use it to determine your best study method and then stop. Some popular charting methods include:

- Begin studying several days before an exam.

- Organize notes so they are easy to review.

- Use self-testing as a way to determine whether your current study method is effective.

- Adapt your study plan for each type of test.

Review Objectives of the Class before Each Study Session

Instructors will provide you with a list of objectives when starting a course. You should keep this list and review it before each study session. This list will help you determine what areas will be the most vital.

Many instructors will even provide students with an advance organizer before each lesson. An advance organizer is either in the form of a verbal statement or a visual representation that is designed to give students a sense of where the lesson is going and lists important things they will need to learn by the end of each lesson. If your instructor provides this, write it down and review it before each study session.

Get Organized

Lack of organization is the number one cause of low academic performance, which means that you must stay organized. By this point in your Air Force career, the need for organization will have been drilled into your head. You will find yourself facing many different instructors and classes. All of this can quickly become overwhelming if you don't keep it sorted out.

Here are some tips that will help you bring order to this chaos:

 ➢ **Use a separate notebook for each class.** Take it a step further and use a different color notebook for every class.

 ➢ **Take notes.** If the instructors allows you to tape their class using an audio recorder then do it.

 ➢ **Backpacks make it easier to keep up with your supplies.** Make sure that you check your backpack every day, ensuring that you have everything that you will need throughout the day packed.

➢ **Carry a schedule book** to keep up with quizzes for each class. That way you are never surprised – unless there is a pop quiz.

➢ **Make sure that you keep your study area equipped with a lot of pens, pencils, and printer ink.**

Develop a Plan to Prepare for Tests

Aside from your organizational skills and study methods, here are a few more tips that will help you prepare for tests.

➢ Cramming is an unhealthy habit, yet so many people brag about their ability to cram for an exam. Cramming forces you to overwhelm your mind with a ton of information too quickly. It's extremely stressful and will lead to anxiety for future tests. Plus, it makes you absolutely hate testing altogether.

➢ As mentioned earlier in this chapter, try out different strategies for studying and then choose the ones that are right for you.

➢ Always consider that all tests are different. For example, multiple choice tests are a lot different than essay tests. Therefore, you will have to prepare for each one differently. For an essay test, you would probably review concepts and prepare an outline for possible questions while multiple choice tests would require you to review notes and reread passages of your textbook.

> Use self-testing as a guide to determine what areas need your attention the most.

> Take time to write down ideas that you feel might be a part of the upcoming test.

What to Do on Test Day

Preparation is a very important part of acing your next test but what you do on test day is equally as important. What you do on test day is what will ultimately determine your performance. After all, you can prepare until you're blue in the face but if you do not put that preparation to practical use then it's essentially worthless. With that said, here's what you can do on test day to improve your score.

> Budget your time appropriately. Know how long you have to take the test and pay attention to the clock.

> Take a moment to glance over the entire test before starting so that you know what to expect.

> Always finish the easier sections first. The more you get out of the way early, the more time you will have remaining to tackle the tougher sections.

> Read the directions carefully.

> Read each question carefully before answering.

> Don't be afraid to ask a question if you do not understand what a question is asking.

Surviving Tests

➢ Keep a steady pace.

➢ If you don't know the answer to a question, skip it and come back to it later. Who knows? Another question might spark your memory.

➢ Change positions every once in a while in order to relax.

➢ If students start turning in their tests and you still have a lot remaining then never panic. It's not a race. There's no extra credit for turning in a test early so it's better to take as much time as needed to get it right.

➢ Essay questions can be intimidating so if you get stuck, choose a question and just start writing. It will help spark your mind and get you on the right track.

Chapter 6

Using the Chain of Command

One of the most important aspects of the Air Force is its structure. It's absolutely vital that you understand how this structure operates. It all starts with the Chain of Command.

Air Force Chain of Command

The Air Force chain of command is designed to promote control and communication in the most efficient manner possible. Every link in this chain has its own level of responsibility. It extends from the lowest rank, all the way up to the Commander in Chief (President of the United States). Every level has specific responsibilities and authority. There are a few things that every link in the Chain of Command has in common.

Every level of the Air Force Chain of Command is responsible for all lower levels, and held accountable by all higher levels.

The Chain of Command will not work without dedication from every level. As the saying goes, a chain is only as strong as its weakest link. Everyone has an important role to play in the Chain of Command and you are expected to follow it correctly.

Using the Chain of Command

Some people mistakenly believe that following this chain is like following a corporate ladder but the two are completely different. Whereas in the civilian world you might get away with going above your boss's head to resolve a problem, you need to be extremely careful about doing that in the Air Force. More often than not, your Commanding Officer will be able to resolve any problems that you might have.

Always resolve problems at the lowest possible level.

Never, under any circumstances, should you skip a level; request assistance at the lowest possible level before moving to the next. In some cases, you will get referred to the higher level. With that said, let's look at some of the ranks in more detail.

First Sergeant

The position of First Sergeant is time honored position that is critical to the success of missions. First Sergeants are not generally required to possess a specific technical expertise but they must be able to understand the importance of their decisions.

A First Sergeant supports subordinates through management and support of all Airmen under their command. He/she works directly for the unit Commander, serving as an essential link between the commander and unit. A First Sergeant's job is to make sure that all of the Commanding

Officer's goals, policies, and objectives are understood by the Airmen under his command. Furthermore, a First Sergeant also ensures that agencies within the base are quick to respond to the needs of Airmen and their families.

Command Chief Master Sergeant (CCM)

The CCM monitors, advises, and then ensures that the Commanding Officer's policies are all carried out. CCMs are advisors who are very important to the Chain of Command. A CCM provides pivotal advice and recommendations to the Commanding Officer for all matters relating to enlisted personnel.

A CCM will build a senior non-commissioned officer (SNCO) support channel that consists of other enlisted leaders like:

➢ Other CCMs

➢ Career Field Managers

➢ Functional Area Managers

➢ Group Superintendents

➢ Commandants

➢ First Sergeants

This support group does not replace the established Chain of Command. It supports the established Chain of Command. A CCMs job is also to be the driving force behind the training and development of enlisted personnel.

Using the Chain of Command

Those are the two important positions in the Air Force that you will need to know about. We will not go into detail about all of the other positions since this book is dedication to getting you through your first year in the Air Force. Just remember that if hope to survive your first year then you must effectively utilize this Chain of Command. Always take your problems to the lowest position possible to seek advice.

Staff Agencies

There are more than just individual positions that support and strengthen the Air Force. There are also agencies that are utilized to strengthen the Chain of Command. These agencies include:

- Chaplain

- Staff Judge Advocate

- Equal Opportunity

- Sexual Assault Prevention

- Response Program

- Inspector General

These agencies all provide critical advice and assistance in different areas of the Air Force. They do not substitute for the Chain of Command, but provide support that makes it much more efficient and effective. So let's take a moment to go through thee agencies before wrapping up this chapter.

Chaplain

The Chaplain Corps help Airmen and their families exercise their constitutional right to freedom of religion. This is done through a carefully prepared system of religious observances and confidential counseling. The overall goal is to discover and advise the Commanding Officer of any spiritual, ethical, moral, core values, and religious accommodation issues that might come up from time-to-time.

Staff Judge Advocate (SJA)

The SJA provides legal services as they are needed by Commanders and other Staffing Agencies. This agency closely monitors and advises Commanders on legal issues that might creep up sometimes. They also review all policies on a regular basis to ensure that they meet any revised laws. The SJA also provides legal assistance to Airmen and their families.

Uniform Code of Military Justice (UCMJ)

Since the military environment is unique, it needs to be governed by its own justice agency. The United States Air Force serves all around the world so it requires a very unique set of laws to ensure good order and discipline.

You will quickly learn that this might be the most important agency in the Air Force. It will help protect your constitutional rights while ensuring that offenders are held accountable for their actions. You need to regularly review

Using the Chain of Command

the UCMJ rules and regulations so that you know any changes.

Finally, even though you are going to be regulated by a special set of military laws, you are still expected to follow all local civilian laws for wherever you are deployed.

Personal Legal Assistance

Each base has a number of legal officers who provide confidential legal assistance for Airmen should you need it. They provide assistance with personal civilian legal matters, which supports command effectiveness. Some legal areas that are covered by Personal Legal Assistance are:

- ➤ Wills
- ➤ Estate Planning
- ➤ Financial Affairs
- ➤ Family Law
- ➤ Consumer Affairs
- ➤ Servicemembers' Civil Relief Act
- ➤ Veterans' Reemployment Rights
- ➤ Taxes

All assistance is subject to availability of the needed resources and expertise. Priority is given to mobilization and deployment related issues.

Public Affairs (PA)

The goal of Public Affairs is to accurately provide useful information about Air Force activities to the Department of Defense in a timely manner. The representative for Public Affairs is appointed by the Commanding Officer and also serves as his personal spokesperson and advisor.

A Public Affairs Officer also helps to provide the Commander with advice on the implications that decisions might have on public opinion. The representative must have the necessary resources to provide the public and media with accurate information in a timely manner.

Equal Opportunity (EO)

The purpose of this program is to enhance the cohesion of the unit by making sure that all Airmen are treated equally and fairly. The Air Force has a zero-tolerance policy towards discrimination that is against the law – including but not limited to sexual harassment. When a case of discrimination is alleged, action will be taken immediately. This process starts with an investigation that will look deeper into the discrimination.

Using the Chain of Command

Remember that you are never allowed to discriminate against another member of the Air Force. This includes discriminating behavior based on:

- ➢ Race
- ➢ Color
- ➢ Religion
- ➢ Gender
- ➢ National Origin
- ➢ Age
- ➢ Disability
- ➢ Reprisal
- ➢ Genetic Information

The EO office will assist with any discrimination issues by providing information, assessing the problem, providing resolution services, and the advising Commanding Officers of their findings. If you feel that you are being discriminated against, then don't hesitate to visit the EO office and see what your options are.

Although enforcing laws is not an EO matter, they take the first steps into investigating these cases. Allegations of discrimination can also be made to the Unit Commander or the Inspector General.

11 Simple Tools to Survive your First Year in the Air Force

The Inspector General (IG)

The IG serves as the eyes and ears of the Commanding Officer. His job is to be alert and notice any issues that might affect the organization as a whole. The Inspector General has so many responsibilities that it has to be organized into two separate systems: The Air Force Inspection System and the Air Force Complaints Resolution Program. Let's take a quick look at each of those systems.

The Air Force Inspection System

The Air Force Inspection System's job is to ensure that the unit is efficient, effective, ready for operation, and follows all guidelines. It is not limited to a single area but encompasses all aspects of the Air Force and extends to all levels of command.

The Air Force Complaints System

The Air Force Complains System provides all Airmen with an outlet to report complaints without a fear of reprisal. This is to protect the constitutional rights of all members of the Air Force. Complaints are allowed to be submitted either in person, by phone, in writing, or through email. You are always allowed to use this system since it's a right protected by law. Keep this in mind during your career in the Air Force since many new Airmen do not file complaints under fear of reprisal.

Note: You should always attempt to resolve complaints at the lowest possible level before you use this channel. In most

Using the Chain of Command

cases, issues can be resolved by your Commanding Officer.

In addition to being given rights, all members of the United States Military have a duty to report any forms of fraud, waste, abuse, and mismanagement of any kind.

Chapter 7

Air Force Entitlements

Airmen are sometimes eligible for different types of pay in addition to their basic pay, depending on their circumstances. This section will look at some of this special pay.

Medical and Dental Officer Pay
Medical and dental officers receive special pay according to how many years they have been in service. This amount can be anywhere from $5,000 to $15,000 per year.

Board certified medical officers can receive anywhere from $4,000 to $31,000 per year.

Optometrists and Veterinarians
Eligible for $100 per month of extra incentive pay.

Special Duty Pay
Enlisted airmen who are performing designated special duties will receive a bonus ranging from $55 to $375 per month. The amount received is dependent on the level of the special duty. A prime example of special duty assignments is a recruiter.

Air Force Entitlements

Overseas Extension Pay
Depending on the location and job, airmen can receive up to $80 per month for voluntarily extending their duty in an overseas area.

Aviation Continuation Pay
This bonus is available to aviation officers who fall below the paygrade of O-6. If they extend their service obligation then they will receive a bonus ranging from $4,000 to $6,000 per year.

Engineering and Scientific Officer Continuation Pay
A bonus of $3,000 per year can be paid to commissioned officers who serve as engineers and scientists if they extend their service commitment.

Foreign Duty Pay
Enlisted airmen who are stationed outside of the continental United State can receive foreign duty pay. This amount varies depending on rank and can be as high as $22.50 per month. It's also worth noting that an individual will not receive this bonus if they are stationed in a state/country where they are a resident. For example, an airman who resides in Alaska cannot receive this bonus if they are stationed in Alaska.

Foreign Language Proficiency Pay
Airmen who are proficient in a foreign language and are assigned to a job that requires this skill are eligible for a

bonus ranging from $25 to $100. This amount is completely dependent on the Airman's level of proficiency.

Aviation Retention Bonus Pay
Aviation Officers who make a written commitment to remain on active duty beyond their initial commitment can receive a bonus ranging from $6,000 to $25,000 per year. This amount is determined by how many additional years they commit to.

Flight Pay
This special pay is reserved for airmen who are required to log frequent and regular aircraft flights. It ranges from $150 to $250 per month.

Hazardous Duty Pay
Do not mistake this for "Hostile Fire Pay". Hazardous Duty Pay is a bonus paid to airmen who perform duties that are hazardous. This can include parachuting, demolition duty, or any duties that involve toxic chemicals. The bonus is $150 per month.

Family Separation Allowance
Airmen who are separated from their legal dependents for at least 30 days are eligible for a family separation allowance. This is only applicable when an Airman is assigned to a location where their dependent is not authorized to accompany him/her. There are actually two types of family separation allowances and military personnel can get both.

Air Force Entitlements

They are FSA-1 and FSA-2.

FSA-1 is payable when a member cannot reside on base at their new assignment. This payment is designed to help pay for rent and utilities that are associated with having two households. The payment is equal to the basic allowance for housing rate.

FSA-2 is payable when the member is separated from legal dependents for at least 30 days. The amount is $250 per month.

Combat Pay

This bonus is paid when an airman is deployed into a combat zone. The rate is $225 per month. Furthermore, being assigned to a combat zone also triggers a tax advantage.

Clothing Allowance

There are two different types of clothing allowances: annual maintenance and initial clothing allowance. Initial clothing allowance is paid when the military is not able to issue an Airman's initial uniforms. The amount received depends on the cost of uniform items and differs for men and women.

Special Personal Allowance

Anyone in the military who is in certain *special positions* can receive a personal allowance that is designed to help with incidental and entertainment expenses.

11 Simple Tools to Survive your First Year in the Air Force

Severance Pay

Airmen who have served at least 6 years (but less than 20) are eligible for severance pay if they receive an honorable discharge. This only applies when the discharge is involuntary. The amount is equal to 10% of their annual base pay multiplied by the number of years they have been in service.

Hardship Duty Pay

Airmen who are station at specific *hardship* locations are eligible for Hardship Duty Pay that ranges from $50 to $700 per month.

Retirement Pay

Serving at least 20 years in the military means that you can retire, receiving a portion of your base pay every month for the rest of your life.

Reenlistment Bonuses

The purpose of offering a reenlistment bonus is to offer an incentive for members to reenlist for positions that might be experiencing a critical shortage. For the Air Force, this bonus can be as high as $60,000! Here's how it works:

Generally speaking, the higher the reenlistment bonus, the harder the time that the Air Force is having with filling the position. This is generally because either:

Air Force Entitlements

1. The same job is being offered to civilians at a much higher wage. This causes people to leave the military to take more money.

2. The job is undesirable.

Half of the reenlistment bonus is generally paid at the time of reenlistment and the rest is paid through annual installments. Congress has given the military the option of paying the entire bonus in one lump sum and depending on how badly the position needs to be filled, the Air Force might decide to use that option.

Generally speaking, it's not a good idea to seek jobs based on pay alone. Even a lump sum of money as incentive will be gone after a short time. Base every decision on your personal preferences. If a job opens up that you truly want and it comes attached with an incentive then by all means, take it!

Tax Benefits

Generally speaking, all military base pay is taxable while allowances are not. Different states have different laws for taxing military personnel. Let's look at some of the basics so you have a better idea of what to expect.

Chapter 8

Maintain your Fiscal Health

Life in the Air Force has a lot of similarities to civilian life. You still have a regular job (mostly classes if you're still in your first year), bills, housing, and other responsibilities that come with everyday life. You will be working with other people, have a boss, and have to show initiative if you want to advance.

With that said, military life has a lot more responsibility. There is always a chance that you could get deployed into a combat zone. You have to always be on time for work – there are no excuses for being late. If you're late, you get punished. You always have to be carefully groomed to meet military standards. There is even a specific way that you have to talk to others. It's not just a job; you are committing to the protection of the United States.

Therefore, you don't want financial concerns weighing you down. Civilian life does pay more than the military but there is a catch – you have to pay for your own benefits most of the time. You have to spend money on health insurance, education, housing, moving, and even travel.

In the military, you have all of that stuff taken care of, for the most part. Before we get into all of the financial stuff, let's compare life in the military to civilian life.

Air Force Life vs. Civilian Life

Pay

Military: Military pay has several tax advantages and also includes incentives like special pay and allowances.

Civilian: Civilian pay is generally a tad higher than military but there are usually not as many tax advantages as there is with military pay.

Health Care

Military: There are a lot of health care options with the military, including full health coverage that you do not pay for. This free coverage is only available while on active duty.

Civilian: Your health care options depend on the employer but more often than not, individuals are

Housing

Military: Housing is provided by the military if you live on base. If you live off base, then you are generally granted a basic allowance for housing that is exempt from taxes.

Life Insurance

Military: Provided all life insurance coverage free of charge.

Civilian: Civilians must purchase their own life insurance

Education

Military: The GI Bill covers college and graduate education for officers, but there are endless possibilities for improvement through education.

Civilian: Civilians are responsible for their own education. They are at the mercy of scholarships and

Vacation Time

Military: Thirty days guaranteed vacation every year, unless deployed.

Civilian: Most employers start out by providing 5-10 days per year of paid time off and gradually increase it

Work Hours

Military: Hours vary from week-to-week and military personnel work weekends from time-to-time. However, all military are on call 24 hours a day, 7 days a week.

Civilian: Full-time jobs generally require between 35-50 hours per week.

Retirement Options

Military: Most military personnel can retire after 20 years of active duty. There are some cases where one can retire after only 15 years!

Civilian: Retirement options vary but most employers require one to work at least 35 years before they can

Create a Personal Budget Now!

Seriously, don't put it off another day. Sit down and hammer out a budget today! Sitting down and drawing up a budget can be quite intimidating – so intimidating that only around 40% of American families have a budget. However, it's definitely worth the effort. Budgeting can help you avoid debt and cut expenses.

Here is a quick 10-step process to building your own budget:

1. Know How Much Money you Have

Gather all of your bank statements from any savings, checking, and investment account that you might have. You need to determine just how much money you have. Write it down. Knowing your net worth is important because it gives you a basis for starting your budget.

2. Know your Income

This is a breeze since your military pay is based on rank. You need to determine how much you make per month. Write this amount down.

3. Know your Expenses

Now you need to determine what monthly amounts you owe. This probably won't be too hard since a lot of your expenses are covered and you are not likely to be in debt. Write down all of these monthly reoccurring expenses like:

  ➢ Car Loans

Maintain your Fiscal Health

- ➢ Credit Card Payments
- ➢ Utilities
- ➢ Cell Phone

4. Calculate your Net Worth

Your net worth is the total amount of money that you make minus the total amount that you have to pay. This is an eye-opener! You would be surprised at how many people discover that they have a negative net worth. I very seriously doubt that you're going to have a negative net worth since you are just starting out with your career in the Air Force but it's important to know exactly where you stand.

5. Calculate Your Average Recurring Monthly Expenses

This can be a difficult task for many people. The best method of determining your monthly expenses is to collect all of your expenses for a month and then divide these bills into categories. You can be as specific or generic as you want here. Some bill categories might include automotive, household expenses, etc. Determine your average expense per category.

6. Enter All of your Information into a Ledger

Today, we have amazing budgeting tools like Microsoft Excel or online tools like Mint. My point is that it's much easier to keep up with a budget in today's world than it was in the past. Start out by entering all of the information that you have accumulated in the previous steps into a ledger.

7. Pay Attention to the Bottom Line

When you plug all of your information into a budget then you will be able to see the bottom line. This number will determine whether you are overspending or underspending. Ideally, you will discover that you are underspending here. However, if you discover that you're overspending then you must make adjustments to your budget.

8. Make Adjustments to your Budget

If you do determine that you are overspending then you will have to make cuts. There are a ton of resources that will show you some of the best areas to cut. However, I'm sure that most people who are reading this book are underspending. In that case, you should consider investing a portion of that money.

9. Make Adjustment to Categories as Needed

Food gets more expensive and gas goes up so you need to be prepared just in case this happens. Every time you notice inflation, then you will need to add money to categories that might be affected.

10. Be Disciplined

Keeping track of your budget does take some effort. It takes roughly an hour per week but saves much more than that in the long run. One of the greatest powers that a budget holds is that it keeps you motivated. You are able to see the long-

Maintain your Fiscal Health

term results of disciplined financial planning. Therefore, devote an hour every week to keeping your budget up to date.

Chapter 9

Getting to Know the System

In the Air Force, your image matters. Like it or not, people will base their first impression of you on the way you're dressed. As an airman, the way you appear reflects not just yourself, but the Air Force itself. Therefore, your appearance matter whether you are on-duty, or off-duty. It's not just about the clothes you wear either. It goes much deeper than that. I can promise you that if you are caught reflecting a poor image off-duty then it's going to affect your military career. Let's look at some of the principles that the Air Force requires.

Your Personal Appearance Matters!

You should always take pride in your appearance. This is actually true for any profession but in the Air Force, you are always required to maintain a professional appearance. Your appearance is always judged by five factors:

> Cleanliness

> Safety

> Neatness

> Uniformity

> Military Image

Getting to Know the System

While military image can be quite subjective, the other elements are absolutes. The reason the Air Force places such a high value on the way its airmen dress is because civilians draw their conclusions from what they see. If they see an active airman wearing torn and dirty clothing, then they are going to see the whole Air Force as unprofessional.

Here are a couple more rules that are not commonly known. Don't worry, you will learn these quickly while at basic training!

➢ When in uniform, Airmen cannot have their hands in their pockets unless they are either placing or removing an item.

➢ While in an official capacity, Airmen cannot engage in public displays of affection. There are a few exceptions (howbeit brief) such as departure or upon return from being deployed.

➢ Airmen cannot use tobacco products while in uniform, unless they are in a designated smoking area.

➢ Airmen cannot consume any food or beverages while they are walking in uniform. The only exception to this rule is made by a commanding officer.

➢ While walking in uniform, Airmen cannot use personal electronic devices unless it's for an emergency. However, a commanding officer can authorize the use of headphones during physical training. This is only applicable when wearing an authorized PT uniform.

Always Stay Well Groomed

The Air Force has strict rules regarding personal grooming. While there are a few minor variations allowed for women, all airmen must comply with these guidelines. Commanding officers and supervisors also have the ability to determine whether an airman meets these guidelines.

Tattoos

The Air Force does not allow tattoos anywhere on the body that might be seen as obscene or associated with any extremist organization. This includes anything that might come across as religious discrimination. Anyone who might have an unauthorized tattoo is required to have it altered or removed. Furthermore, tattoos should not be in a location where they can be seen while in uniform.

Excessive tattoos are also not allowed. The U.S. Air Force defines excessive as anything that covers over 25% of the body.

Body Piercings

Regardless of whether or not you're in uniform, when in a military installation you are not allowed to wear any piercings. The only exception is for women, who are allowed to wear earrings when off-duty. However, women are limited to one earring per ear.

Getting to Know the System

Uniforms

The Air Force uniform is designed to be plain and distinctive. It identifies you as a member of the United States Air Force so you are carrying a tradition when wearing this uniform. All airmen must:

➢ Acquire all required uniform items.

➢ Follow all rules regarding wearing the uniform.

➢ Keep their uniforms clean, neat, and buttoned.

➢ Know all of the authorized uniform combinations.

➢ Know exactly where to place any ribbons or insignia.

During official military duty, Airmen are required to wear their uniforms unless they are given permission to wear civilian clothing. Any Airmen who are assigned to unofficial Air Force organization must wear the Air Force equivalent uniform to meet the dress code of the organization. Even if you are given permission to wear civilian clothing while on duty, you must still comply with the Air Force code for personal appearance.

Remember that you must dress appropriately for travel.

You are allowed to wear any combination of uniform, except for your flight duty uniform, when arriving and departing from any commercial airport. When departing from or arriving at a military airfield, all combinations of uniform are okay. Under certain circumstances, you will be allowed to wear civilian clothing during travel. Even if it's allowed, you must ensure that your clothing is neat and clean.

When dressing for social functions, you must wear the proper attire as requested by the host or hostess of the function. If you wear your uniform to a civilian social event, then you should wear one of the following:

➢ Service Dress Uniform

➢ Mess Dress Uniform

➢ Semiformal Uniform

➢ Formal Uniform

You are prohibited from wearing your Air Force uniform under any of the following situations:

➢ When attending an event that is sponsored by any group who the Attorney General of the United States officially considers fascist, totalitarian, communist, or subversive.

➢ When attending any public political demonstration that's purpose is to approve opposition of the United States military.

➢ Any situation that would discredit the United States military.

➢ When you are attempting to further your personal career or commercial interests are at stake.

Getting to Know the System

> If you are a defendant in civilian court and the conviction could discredit the Air Force.

You are not allowed to wear distinctive items with your civilian clothing under any circumstances. Distinctive items are defined as those that are unique to your uniform. This includes ribbons, grade insignias, cap devices, and uniform jackets.

Air Force Physical Fitness Ongoing Physical Fitness Requirements

You might believe that basic training will mark the end of your grueling physical training but that is not the case. Physical fitness is going to be an ongoing concern, which is why you should get started as soon as possible. Always maintain an active lifestyle that keeps your body fit. Basic training will help you get into the habit of staying physically fit but it will become your responsibility to maintain that level of fitness.

The Air Force requires its members to be physically fit so that they can support an Air Force mission at any given time. By living an active lifestyle, you will increase your productivity, optimize your health, and maintain a higher level of readiness should you get called to deployment. This will also lead to you projecting the proper military image.

You will be required to submit for fitness assessments in order to determine your overall fitness level. Your age and gender are taken into consideration.

Commanders and supervisors will generally include fitness as part of their organizational culture to help maintain the right level of fitness. Even though you will probably be a part of some on the job fitness training, I highly recommend that you continue to use the gym and other facilities to ensure that you are in optimal shape. Your fitness is your responsibility.

Housing

Yes, your housing is a direct part of your professional appearance. As an Airman, you will be expected to keep your home organized and clean. While you are allowed (in most cases) to choose where you live, your home must still always remain clean and orderly. Yes, even if you personally own the home you will still be expected to follow this rule. Besides, it just makes good sense to keep your home clean.

Conduct

Everyone in the Air Force is part of a very important national defense mission. All Airmen have a serious responsibility to carry out that mission at all times. Your responsibility includes following orders and maintaining all of the high standards set by the Air Force. Maintaining good order and discipline is paramount to completing this mission.

The core value set for all Airmen is that you treat others with respect, fairness, and dignity at all times. Every member of the Air Force is entitled to be treated in a fair and unbiased manner. They are also expected to return this respectful behavior. Always respect these core values. Respect everyone, no matter their race, color, religion, gender, national origin, age, disability, or sexual orientation. Even though you might not agree with their lifestyle, you should still respect that person.

These core values are not limited to personal interactions either. They extend to all communications, including social media. Your goal should always be to never degrade the public's trust I the United States Air Force.

Personal and Professional Relationships Matter

Every decision you make reflects on the Air Force so you need to choose healthy personal relationships. Since the Air Force is not going to be monitoring every choice you make, it's your responsibility to pursue healthy relationships. If a relationship starts to adversely affect you then it becomes an official concern. Unhealthy relationships have the ability to affect your performance, respect for authority, and even the ability to accomplish your mission. As a member of the Air Force, you must choose your personal relationships with care.

All professional relationships should be formed with the Air Force core values in mind. These core values are:

➢ Integrity First

➢ Service Before Self

➤ Excellence In All We Do

Professional relationships can be formed over the phone, face-to-face, and even through social media. Developing professional relationships with other Air Force personnel is vital to your survival. It helps the maximize productivity which plays a huge role in the effective operation of the Air Force.

Unlike in the civilian workforce, the fact that maintaining a professional relationship with another member of the Air Force might be difficult is no excuse. You are still expected to maintain the highest standards of the Air Force.

Relationships Between Superiors and Subordinates
There are very strict rules that you need to know about developing relationships with a superior or subordinate. There is a very delicate balance of appropriateness that must always be maintained. Let's start by discussing social interaction.

All social interaction that encourages the unit to be more effective is not only allowed, but it's encouraged. This can happen wither while on-duty or off-duty. In most cases this type of interaction would have to include all members of the unit.

However, any form of relationship is considered unprofessional is it could be taken as a show of favoritism.

Getting to Know the System

Officers and enlisted personnel cannot fraternize if it can be taken as a show of favoritism.

They cannot form personal relationships at all. There are no exceptions: not on the phone, social media, or any electronic means.

Fraternization is a crime committed when a personal relationship is formed between an officer and an enlisted member. The relationship doesn't necessarily have to be of a romantic nature either. Excessive socialization, even perceived, can degrade leadership because other subordinates might feel that they are being treated unfairly.

With the boom in digital technologies available to us all, maintaining professional relationships without crossing the line should be a primary concern. It's easy to cross that line if you're not paying attention. When this balance is not strictly maintained, then it can:

> Weaken the position of authority within ranks

> Jeopardize group relationships

> Lead to a concern of unequal treatment

> Cause job performance to suffer

> Lower the morale of a unit

In regards to Joint Service operations, the same rules apply since they can still have an impact on all of the above. So an Officer from the Air Force cannot fraternize with a subordinate from the Army.

Finally, since civilian employees and contractors are an important part of the Air Force, military personnel must maintain professional relationships with them. Civilians contribute directly to the success of the mission.

Bullying is Not Tolerated in the Air Force

Inflicting any kind of harm on another Airman is not going to be tolerated. This isn't high school anymore! Bullying includes any instance where you might physically or psychologically abuse another person. Bullying includes degrading, dehumanizing, or even injuring another Airman. Supervisors and Commanders will keep an eye out for any form of this behavior.

Air Force Ethics

All Airmen are expected to uphold an extremely high standard of conduct and integrity. This not only includes your job, but all of your relationships with people both professionally and personally. If your behavior creates even the slightest appearance of impropriety then you're going to get into trouble. Here is a quick look at the Federal Regulations that you will be required to follow:

> ➢ Service in the military means that you must act in a way where you maintain the public's trust. So you

Getting to Know the System

must place loyalty to the Constitution and laws above personal gain at all times.

➤ Airmen cannot sell government information or condone the improper use of it.

➤ Airmen cannot accept any gifts or money from people who are seeking official action. There are a few exceptions to this rule including:

- Modest amounts of food or drink that is not part of a meal.

- Presentation items that have little intrinsic value. Some examples include trophies, certificates, and plaques.

- Discounts that are offered to all military personnel.

- Items that are worth $20 or less. However, not more than $50 worth of items can be taken from a single source in a calendar year.

- Gifts that are based on personal relationships.

➤ Airmen must always give their fullest effort to perform all of their duties.

➤ Airmen can't make unauthorized commitments or promises that bind the government.

➤ Airmen cannot ever use their public appointment for private gain.

11 Simple Tools to Survive your First Year in the Air Force

➤ Always be impartial and never give preferential treatment to a private organization or individual.

➤ Protect and conserve Federal property.

➤ Never use Federal property in any way that is unauthorized.

➤ Airmen cannot seek outside employment that is in conflict with official government responsibilities.

➤ Airmen are required to satisfy all financial obligations.

➤ Always follow all laws regarding equal opportunity for all Americans. Race, color, religion, sex, national origin, age, and handicap status can never be taken into account.

➤ Avoid all actions that might create the appearance of violating local laws or ethical military standards.

➤ Higher ranking military personnel are not allowed to solicit to you as a junior. The only exception is for the one-time sale of personal property. Some examples include a house or a vehicle. However, as the junior officer, you would have to approach him/her and you would receive fair market value.

➤ Gambling of any kind is not allowed while on-duty or on any government owned property unless the activity is authorized.

➤ Airmen cannot endorse (or even appear to endorse)

fundraising for any charity. There are a few exceptions to this rule like Combined Federal Campaigns or other military approved fundraisers.

Requirements as Members of a Private Organization

Airmen who work part-time at a professional organization then you have a few rules that you must follow. I doubt many of you reading this book will choose to work part-time since most will have to put their full focus on Air Force duties and studies. So I will keep this section short. When working for a professional organization, you must follow these rules:

➤ You cannot use your title and/or position in the Air Force in a way that suggests it endorses the organization.

➤ It must not interfere with your duties as an Airman.

Performance of Duties

It is always your number one responsibility to carry out your duties and accomplish the mission. However, it takes much more than technical proficiency to accomplish the mission. You will learn how to be a team player. You will learn how to be responsible for your duties and accomplish them in an efficient manner. Airmen are always held accountable for their own actions so if you have a bad habit of making excuses, you'll have to break that habit. Supervisors and Commanders will monitor you much more closely than any boss in the civilian world.

11 Simple Tools to Survive your First Year in the Air Force

All Airmen are expected to be good teammates. Quality and quantity are equally as important since the Air Force measures both. You will quickly notice a lot of huge differences in civilian jobs and Air Force jobs.

Wingmen

All Airmen have a role as Wingmen. The idea is that a Wingman will safeguard his/her lead and that a lead will never allow his/her Wingman to get into danger. This concept is an essential aspect of the Air Force and will get drilled into your head time after time until it becomes common practice. You will be required to always protect your fellow Airmen and take action when needed. This is not only true for the mission, but in everyday life.

If you notice that a fellow Airman is about to make a poor decision, then you are expected to step in and help him/her. It is always your responsibility to watch over your companions.

Commanding Officers will also recognize when those under their command need help. They are the first line of defense for the well-being of those under their command. Don't be afraid to ask for help if needed, especially from your Commanding Officer. It often takes more courage to ask for help rather than facing a difficult situation alone. In your first year, you might just need that help.

Getting to Know the System

Drug Abuse is not Tolerated

Using illegal drugs, in any profession, is simply something you cannot do. Illegal drug use is defined as the use of any type of drug that is not prescribed. I won't get into the specifics of illegal drugs since it's covered in the common sense department. Any substance that is taken to alter your mood is considered an illegal drug. Legal use of alcohol and tobacco are exceptions.

Intoxicating substances hinder your ability to complete the Air Force overall mission. They seriously damage your health and can jeopardize not only your safety, but the safety of others. If you are caught using illegal drugs, then you can receive a less than honorable discharge and criminal prosecution.

Get Help Immediately!

Airmen who have a substance abuse problem are encouraged to seek help from their Commanding Officer. There is an Alcohol and Drug Abuse Prevention and Treatment Program that will help. In fact, you might be required to participate in this program as part of your training. If you have a problem then seeking help will minimize the negative consequences of substance abuse. You can even restore your status to active duty if you go out and seek help. This includes both illegal drugs and the abuse of legal drugs like alcohol. Your Commanding Officer will be much more willing to help you if you go to him/her first, rather than getting caught and then seeking help.

Fiscal Health is Just as Important as Physical Health

This is an area where the military world varies greatly from the civilian world. Not very many civilian jobs care about your personal finances. In the Air Force, your fiscal fitness is considered just as important as your physical fitness. Here are some of the financial requirements as a member of the Air Force:

➢ You are expected to review all statements on a regular basis and make sure that everything is accurate.

➢ You must file all vouchers on a timely basis.

➢ You are expected to pay all of your debts on time.

➢ Develop and maintain a personal budget.

➢ Use credit cards in a responsible manner.

➢ Avoid high interest, short term credit agreements like car title loans.

➢ Support all dependents.

Satisfying these financial obligations is not optional – it's a requirement to meet the Air Force standards of conduct. If you need help, then the Air Force will provide you will financial management information, personal counseling, and legal assistance.

Getting to Know the System

All Airmen Must Make Dependent Care Arrangements Ahead of Time

The Air Force mission requires that people be in the right place at the right time. All Airmen are expected to be ready to perform their duty at a moment's notice. There are no excuses. All Airmen must be ready to deploy at a moment's notice so it is your responsibility to be sure that you plan in advance for the care of all dependents. Make arrangements as soon as possible just in case you have to deploy.

You can either set up arrangements with civilian resources or use those available through the military. In fact, I encourage you to have a plan in writing so you know exactly what to do. This plan should cover all possible scenarios, including short term and long term care. Detail it in a way that provides you with a smooth transition during your absence.

This is much easier with married couples than it is for single parents, who will face additional challenges. Even if you are a single parent, you must still be available for deployment on short notice. The key is to plan in advance.

Religion and the Air Force

All members of the United States Air Force have an obligation to protect the Constitutional rights of all American citizens. That includes an individual's right to exercise their religion. Airmen are not allowed to use their position to promote their own personal religious beliefs or give preferential treatment to anyone who follows the same religion. This is mostly applicable to Commanders, but it's good practice for all Airmen to follow this example.

That does not mean that members of the Air Force are not allowed to pursue their own religious beliefs. It just means that they must not allow their pursuit of religion to degrade other denominations. In fact, supporting the free exercise of religion is one of the Air Force's core values and helps to build trust within the team.

> ➤ Airmen are allowed to choose and practice their own religion so long as they respect others whose viewpoints might differ from their own.

> ➤ Your religious rights do not exclude you from following orders and complying with directives from your superiors.

> ➤ You are allowed to request religious accommodations. However, these requests can be denied by your Commanding Officer.

Politics and the Air Force

Generally speaking, you have the same rights as all other United States citizens. However, you are also a member of the Air Force so there are certain restrictions in the way you are allowed to exercise your rights. First and foremost, as a group, the military must always be politically neutral. Here are the rules that you will be required to follow:

Getting to Know the System

➢ As an American citizen, you have the right to vote. In fact, it's your duty to vote.

➢ You **are** allowed to express your political opinion so long as it cannot be taken as an implication that it is a representation of that of the Air Force.

➢ Commissioned Officers, under law, **are not** allowed to use derogatory words against any elected government official. This includes via social media.

➢ You **are** allowed to attend political rallies so long as you are not in uniform.

➢ You **are not** allowed to engage in any kind of political campaign in any manner, regardless of whether or not you are in uniform.

➢ You **are** allowed to make a monetary contribution to a political organization.

➢ You **are** allowed to endorse a political candidate by displaying a bumper sticker on your personally owned vehicles.

➢ You **are not** allowed to display any form of political sign and/or banner in your office, work area, or on-base residence – even if that house is a part of a privatized housing development.

➢ You **are not** allowed to participate in any political demonstration while on a military installation. The only exception is events that are approved by the installation's Commanding Officer.

➢ You **are not** allowed to engage in political discussions in any Federal workplace since it can be seen as an attempt to influence the position of others. The only exception is encouragement to participate in voting.

Authorized Use of Social Media

In today's digitally driven world, there are a lot of different ways to communicate with other people. Text messaging, email, and social networking are all popular forms of communication. This section is going to focus on social media, since it tends to be the most misunderstood area when it comes to the military.

Social networking includes all of the following services:

➢ Facebook

➢ Twitter

➢ MySpace

➢ Google Plus

➢ Web Blogs

➢ Forums or Other Messaging Boards

➢ Skype

These are all web-based services that connect users from

around the world and allow them to communicate with each other. You are personally responsible for everything that you say on social media. You must always respect the guidelines laid out by the Air Force pertaining to what you tell others.

The security of operations within the Air Force is vital to the overall mission. Social media is seen by so many that it increases the risk of these lapses in security. If you use your common sense then you're going to be okay. I recommend that you don't talk about anything related to your military life on social media.

Using social media also comes with the risk of discrediting the Air Force through offensive and inappropriate behavior.

➢ Never post pictures where you appear unprofessional.

➢ Always show respect for authority.

➢ Never make negative comments about another Airman.

Make it clear that you are speaking for yourself and that your opinions do not reflect that of the Air Force. Airmen are allowed to discuss their rank when acting in a personal capacity, but you are not allowed to use your rank to imply that the Air Force sanctions your personal opinion. A lot of people cross this line.

Finally, you must follow all civilian laws regarding the use of

11 Simple Tools to Survive your First Year in the Air Force

social media.

Chapter 10

Life in the Air Force

While many people focus on basic training, it is not the end of your journey into the Air Force – it is only the beginning. Once it's over, you are going to find yourself in a brand new world. It's true that there are several similarities between civilian and military life, but there are some major differences as well. Life on-base is going to be much different from civilian life.

Food Allowance

Officers and enlisted military personnel who do not live in dormitories will receive a food allowance that is around $200 a month. The idea is that the government should pick up all costs of feeding its military. It's tradition. This allowance is non-taxable. It is designed to feed the military member – not his/her family. For example, if you have a spouse and you are deployed overseas, then your spouse will not receive this benefit.

Receiving BAS doesn't have anything to do with your marital status. It's a military decision based on one question: is it more beneficial for you to consume meals in the chow hall or outside of chow hall? If you are married and living with your dependents then you are almost guaranteed to receive BAS.

However, if you are married but are not living with your dependents then you might not get BAS. For example, while in basic training you will not receive this benefit since you are going to be consuming all of your means at the chow hall.

Meals, Ready To Eat (MRE)

A book about life in the Air Force (or any branch of the military for that matter) is not complete without mentioning good ole MREs. MREs are sealed and can be eaten either cold or heated up. Each package contains:

- An Entrée (There are a lot of different entrees)
- Side Dish
- Crackers and Cheese
- Desert
- Cocoa Powder
- Snacks

Every year or two, the military does a survey that asks for everyone's favorite MRE. They remove unpopular items from the menu and create new meals.

MREs are not limited to military personnel but can be purchased from almost all military supply stores and camping shops. In fact, they are highly recommended for disaster kits.

Life in the Air Force

Active Duty G.I. Bill

This bill works the same for all active duty service members. You will decide whether you want to join this bill or not during basic training, after you receive an informative briefing about the program. This is a one-time choice and you cannot change your mind later, so choose wisely.

If you do elect to participate in this bill, then your pay is reduced by $100 for a year. In return for this $1,200 investment, you receive educational benefits worth $37,000. But why wait until the briefing to learn about the G.I. Bill? Start deciding now whether or not the investment is worth the payout. In most cases, it is!

In order to use the benefits from the MGIB, you must serve at least two consecutive years of active duty.

If you plan on using the MGIB after separation from active duty, then you have to meet the following requirements:

➤ Must have an honorable separation.

➤ Have at least three years of active duty. All three years must be consecutive, unless you received an honorable discharge for a very specific reason like medical.

➤ Have at least two consecutive years of active duty if your initial enlistment period was for two years or you obligate to serve an additional four years in the reserves.

11 Simple Tools to Survive your First Year in the Air Force

The G.I. Bill pays more when you leave the military than it does while on active duty. When you are on active duty, it only pays the cost of tuition for the course. This causes most people to opt not to use this bill while on active duty. They will opt to use the military's active duty tuition program.

Reserve Montgomery G.I. Bill
This is essentially the same as the Active Duty G.I. Bill with only a few exceptions:

➤ Your military pay is not deducted for this program.

➤ The benefits are not as high as they are with the Active Duty G.I. Bill. You only receive up to $10,000.

➤ You must enlist for a period of at last six years to be eligible.

➤ You can use the benefits immediately following boot camp but the benefits expire if you do not serve your entire contract.

➤ It expires 14 years after you become eligible to receive benefits (boot camp graduation).

Tuition Assistance
The Air Force offers full tuition assistance for courses that are taken by Airmen while on active duty. There are a few limitations to this though.

➤ Only $4,500 per year is given to each airman per year for tuition.

Life in the Air Force

➤ The Air Force only allows $250 per semester hour.

College Degrees and Commissioning Programs

The Air Force is actually the only military branch that issues college credits and degrees. This is done through a fully accredited community college called Community College of the Air Force (CCAF). The CCAF issues fully accredited college transcripts and awards the Associate of Science Degrees to its members of the Air Force in specific educational fields.

Other branches of the military do not actually issue college degrees or award any credits. They only help with tuition and other job related education. As you can imagine, this benefit alone makes the Air Force an extremely popular choice for enlistment.

Health Care

First of all, if your recruiter makes a bold promise that you will get free health for the remainder of your life, then make sure you read this section so you're not completely left out in the dark. In the past, there was free lifetime healthcare for all military retirees and their immediate families but that is not the case nowadays. While the law hasn't necessarily changed, the availability of military hospitals has been downsized dramatically. In addition, the number of doctors and other medical technicians has also declined.

Adding to the existing problem, the number of people seeking military health care through the system has not declined. So the demand is much higher than the supply.

What Does This Mean For You?

The solution has been that many military retirees and their families are seeking health care through other venues like off-base care. I feel compelled to mention that the military health care system is **far better** than most civilian health care plans available today. It's no secret that health care concerns are a sweeping problem across the entire country. Tricare is one of the best health care plans out there and it's only available to military and their families. There are two major complaints about Tricare:

1. Being promised free health care for life has caused many retired veterans to feel as if they were lied to.

2. In the past, when a retiree became eligible for Medicare, they lost their Tricare benefits. That is not the case anymore so long as they are enrolled in Medicare Part B.

I'm not trying to place doubt in your mind. This book is written to prepare you for life in the Air Force. With that said, while in active service, you and your dependents will all receive free medical care under a provision called Tricare Prime. This is very similar to an HMO in that you are appointed to what is known as a "Primary Care Provider."

Life in the Air Force

That provider is usually the on-base hospital. Either way, that primary provider takes care of all medical concerns and if required, will recommend you to a specialist.

Dental Care
Dental care is free to all active military personnel. However, it is not free if you plan on joining the reserve and are not on active duty. For those who do not meet the free requirements, there is a family dental plan that only costs a few dollars per month. Dental care also falls under the Tricare system.

Since Tricare will become such an important part of your life, let's take a closer look at it.

There are Six Types of Tricare Coverage
If you were to ask your parents or grandparents how many types of Tricare coverage there are, they might answer with "three." That's because there have been several new options established over the past few years. Let's take a closer look at all of the types of coverage.

Tricare Prime
This is the option given to all active military personnel and their families. As mentioned above, those under Tricare Prime are assigned to a Primary Care Provider (PCP) which is normally the on-base hospital. In order to see a specialist, you would have to be referred by your PCP.

> ➤ There is no cost or enrollment fees for active military and their families.

> ➤ For retires under the age of 65, the fee is $230 per year (single coverage) or $460 per year (family coverage).

> ➤ Retirees pay a cost share of $12 for outpatient visits, $30 for emergency services, $25 for mental health visits.

> ➤ The maximum catastrophic cap that retired members must pay every year is $3,000.

The latest option that's available under the Tricare Prime option is a Point of Service option. By electing to enroll in the POS option, you can be enrolled in Tricare Prime but use the options listed in the following sections for Tricare Extra or Tricare Standard.

Enrollment is easy. While you can go online and get all of the forms you need, you will have an officer sit down with you early in basic training to help you enroll.

Tricare Extra

While this program does have a lot more flexibility than Tricare Prime, it can result in additional costs. The most appealing aspect is that you do not have to enroll in advance to use Tricare Extra. You can show up at any authorized Tricare Provider, show them your identification card, and receive medical care.

Life in the Air Force

If you decide to ever use this option, then it's worth noting that you will have to pay an annual amount:

> ➤ $150 for individuals

> ➤ $300 for family

Here are some more noteworthy points:

> ➤ Once you pay the deductible, Tricare Extra will pay 85% of the remaining cost of the visit, leaving you with only 15%.

> ➤ If you (or a family member) have to receive impatient care, then you're responsible for $11.45 per day.

> ➤ If you (or a family member) have to receive impatient mental care, then you're responsible for $11.45 per day or a total of $25. Whichever amount is greater.

> ➤ This plan costs more for retirees (not that you have to worry about that anytime soon!) While the deductible is the same, retirees pay higher percentages afterwards.

When using Tricare Extra, you do not have to fill out any forms. The provider does it for you. Additionally, Tricare will pay the provider their portion of the bill – leaving you with only your portion to pay on each visit.

11 Simple Tools to Survive your First Year in the Air Force

Tricare Standard

This option is very close to the old health care program CHAMPUS. While it does provide you with the greatest flexibility, it is the most expensive option. Plus it can become complicated when Tricare and the health care provider disagree on the cost of your visit. Let me explain.

You are allowed to see pretty much any health care provider you want, but you have to be careful because there is a huge stipulation attached. Active duty military must pay a deductible of $150 (single coverage) or $300 (family coverage). Tricare will then pay 80% of remaining costs for the year. However, here's the catch.

If Tricare says that a medical provider is charging you more than they feel it should cost, then that difference comes out of your pocket. There's more!

Under Tricare Extra, the health care provider you use will fill out all forms associated with the costs. Normally, they are not allowed to claim more than Tricare has dictated for the cost. However, there is a loophole around this. If the healthcare provider gets you to sign a separate agreement, then they can charge more. Additionally, you will be responsible for that amount. Most people don't know about this provision so it's important that you pay attention to everything you sign.

Life in the Air Force

Tricare for Reserves

Reserve members fall under a different system – sort of. Reserves can use any of the above Tricare options for themselves and their dependents if they are called to active duty and remain on active duty for at least 30 days. If a service man or woman receives a "delayed effective date" for activation, then their health coverage can be purchased at 90 days prior to their activation. This coverage will remain in effect until 180 days after their activation.

Once that 180 day transition has been reached, they are able to purchase a plan under the Tricare Reserve Select Program.

Tricare for Life

In the past, when a retiree from the military reached 65 years of age, they were taken off Tricare because they were expected to get Medicare. However, Tricare for Life changed all of that. This change enabled retired military personnel and their families to remain covered under the Tricare plan while they are also enrolled in Medicare Part B. The only change is the premium. Tricare will simply pick up any pay that Medicare does not cover.

Medicare does not cover medical services that are provided outside of the United States. However, Tricare for Life does cover these expenses as well, making it a primary form of health insurance for those who choose to reside outside of the United States after retirement, even though individuals must still be enrolled in Medicare Plan B.

Tricare Plus

This program allows individuals to use their Tricare Extra or Tricare for Life benefits at military facilities. However, not all military medical clinics will offer the option to use this coverage. Local commanders make this determination. While there are no enrolment fees, individuals are required to enroll at a recognized medical facility. They must then receive all of their care at the same facility.

Three Ways to Get Medication Through Tricare

There are three different ways that you can receive medication through Tricare:

> **Military Pharmacy:** All medications that are available are listed in the BCF (Basic Core Formally).

> **Tricare Mail Order Pharmacy (TMOP)**

> **Civilian Pharmacy:** If the pharmacy is a part of the Tricare network, then the costs are the same as using a military pharmacy. If not, you will pay full price and be reimbursed by Tricare.

The Truth about VA Care

So many people have a lot of false beliefs about the Veterans Administration. Some are horror stories while others are an over-exaggerated perception of what kind of services military personnel receive. First of all, not all veterans or military retirees can receive free medical care. In order to be eligible, one must meet the following requirements:

> ➢ Have served at least 180 days of military service.

> ➢ Have received an honorable discharge.

> ➢ Have a service related illness, injury, or disability.

> ➢ Fall into a certain poverty range.

The Truth about Commissaries

It's not a rarity for civilians to believe that military retirees can just visit a base commissary and get unrealistic discounts. For example, I've heard people say that they think military can buy a new suit for $20 or a carton of cigarettes for $2. That's simply not true. While you can save a lot of money at the Base Exchange (BX), you are not going to get unrealistic prices. Here's how it really works.

Commissaries are funded by the U.S. Government so they use taxpayer dollars to operate. However, they are required to sell items at the same price that they purchase them – with a 5% surcharge added to help pay for operating costs. Most of this surcharge is used to pay cashiers and stockers.

The standard practice is that the commissary provides an overall savings of roughly 30%. That is a pretty big discount but nowhere near what some civilians believe.

Military Exchanges

Military exchanges are allowed to mark up prices. However, the only government funding they receive is help with transportation and utility costs associated with shipping items overseas. Each branch of the military offers a separate exchange system – the Air Force being known as the Air Force Exchange Service.

Contrary to popular belief, you can sometimes find the same items in civilian stores for a cheaper rate. The main savings comes from the fact that no sales tax is charged with purchases. This can add up over time or when purchasing more expensive items.

One of the biggest complaints received is based on the fact that base exchanges do not offer a lot of non-brand name items. Not everyone can afford to pay premium prices for a new shirt.

In the Air Force (and Army) branches, the exchange is also responsible for the operation of gas stations, liquor stores, food franchises, and theatres found on base. AAFES makes an asserted effort to keep its prices slightly lower than anything found off-base.

The base exchanges are one of the best sources of employment for family members of airmen. Some duty members even work for a base exchange on a part time basis during their off-duty hours to earn some extra money.

Life in the Air Force

Overall, base exchanges are a very important benefit for military members living on base. Just don't count of saving a ton of money while shopping.

MWR Activities

The biggest benefit of the base exchange are Morale, Welfare, and Recreation activities – otherwise known as MWR. MWR facilities do not receive any government funding. They even have to pay their own utility bills! While the overall MWR program at a specific base must operate in the green, one area can operate in the red so long as another picks up the slack. For example, if a club is operating at a loss while a bowling alley is in the green, then that's allowed. With that said, let's look at some of the major MWR activities in more detail. After all, you will not survive in the Air Force without a little R&R.

Recreation Centers

These are often called Community Centers and act as the center of all other activities on base. These centers were originally designed so that airmen could get away from their dorm for a bit. They are now used for anything from live concerts to martial arts classes. You can normally get up to a 10% discount on specific events. Sometimes these Recreation Centers even offer discounts for vacations to places like Vegas and Disney World. It's a good idea to always check here before taking a vacation.

Child Development Centers
This is the on base equivalent of a child care center. They take care of your children for a few hours while you are enjoy a night out. Child Development Centers are much cheaper than their off-base counterparts.

Bowling Alleys
You can find a bowling alley or two on almost every Air Force Base. They are pretty much the same as their off-base counterparts. And even have bowling leagues. Most of them have a snack bar and sometimes offer the most delicious food on base!

Youth Centers
Most Air Force Bases have a youth center that offers recreation activities for children. There are usually sporting, physical fitness, and personal development activities available. Youth centers usually charge a very low monthly fee, as well as additional fees for specific events.

Gymnasiums
Gyms are considered essential so they are allowed to operate off of government appropriated funds. Some of the larger bases are equipped with full-blown fitness facilities. In fact, many of these gyms will put off base gyms to utter shame. There is no reason why you would ever get out of shape.

Life in the Air Force

Hobby Shops

Hobby shops provide an affordable way for you to pursue a hobby. There are generally classes ranging from pottery to auto-repair. Many airmen will turn to a hobby to help them develop additional skills that can lead to supplemental forms of income.

Library

Libraries operate on government funding, just like their off-base counterparts. However, on-base libraries are not generally as stocked as those found off-base. If you find yourself serving overseas though, you might find the on-base library a welcome break.

While I have touched on many of the most popular MWR services that you will find on almost all Air Force bases, keep in mind that your station might vary. It's important that you take advantage of these services.

Chapter 11

Balancing your New Military Life

You will be starting a whole new life in the Air Force. You might have to sacrifice some of your social interests for the achievement of long-term career goals. Several years down the road you will be glad you did!

The transition is not always easy but with a little preparation then you will be able to work through the difficult times. Start out your new life on the right foot by following these basic tips.

> ➤ **You must take responsibility for yourself.** In order to succeed, you must make proactive choices about how to best use your time, resources, and priorities.
> ➤ **Let your values and principles guide you.** Never let others determine what you consider to be important. This should always be based on your own principles.
> ➤ **Prioritize and put important things first.** When you join the military, you are agreeing to put the security of the United States first. That includes putting this security above your own family. Why do you think people always thank the military for their sacrifice?
> ➤ **Discover your key productive times and places.** Some of us are more productive in the morning while others

Balancing your New Military Life

are more productive in the evening.

➤ **You must understand others before you attempt to be understood.** What I mean is that if you have an issue with one of your instructors, you need to put yourself in his/her place. Then ask yourself how you would do it differently. In most cases, you will discover that the issue is with yourself and not the instructor.

➤ **Always seek a better solution.** If you are having problems with a course, then don't just try rereading material. Seek a batter solution like hiring a tutor, meeting with the instructor, or join a study group.

➤ **Never stop challenging yourself.**

Made in the USA
Las Vegas, NV
14 February 2025

18155969R00075